Blessed

FIRST COMMUNION

Dynamic Catholic

Be Bold. Be Catholic.®

My name is

_____

I am blessed, and God made me wonderfully
and marvelously in his own image.
Jesus wants me to become
the-best-version-of-myself,
grow in virtue, and live a holy life.

On this date

_____

I am going to receive the incredible gift of Jesus
during my First Communion.
I am truly blessed.

In accord with the *Code of Canon Law*,
I hereby grant the *Imprimatur* ("Permission to Publish") for *Blessed*.

Most Reverend Dennis M. Schnurr
Archbishop of Cincinnati
Archdiocese of Cincinnati
Cincinnati, Ohio
September 7, 2017

The *Imprimatur* ("Permission to Publish") is a declaration that a book is
considered to be free of doctrinal or moral error. It is not implied that those
who have granted the *Imprimatur* agree with the contents, opinions,
or statements expressed.

Table of Contents

1
Sunday is Special

God, our loving Father,
thank you for all the ways you bless me.
Help me to be aware that every person,
place, and adventure I experience is an
opportunity to love you more.
Fill me with a desire to change and to grow,
and give me the grace to become
the-best-version-of-myself in
every moment of every day.

Amen.

Keep Counting Your Blessings

Welcome. It is time to set out on another great adventure together.

One of the greatest blessings you will ever experience in this life is the Eucharist. So this journey toward your First Communion is very important.

God is inviting you to a great banquet. You are blessed.

You are blessed in so many ways. But every blessing you experience flows from the first blessing. You are a child of God; this is the original blessing.

And now God wants to bless you with the Eucharist!

When you count your blessings before you go to bed tonight, remember to include your favorite foods, the people you love, your talents, your favorite activities and places, and most of all God for giving you all these blessings.

Your Journey with God Continues

We are continuing our journey with God. So, let's review where we have been and where we are going.

Baptism

Before Jesus began his ministry he visited his cousin, John the Baptist, in the desert. John was baptizing many people in the Jordan River to prepare them for the coming of the Messiah.

John encouraged everyone he met to turn back to God, acknowledge their sin, and seek God's forgiveness.

When Jesus arrived at the Jordan River, he asked John to baptize him. At first John refused because he knew that Jesus was the Messiah and, therefore, sinless. But Jesus insisted.

Jesus did not need to be baptized like you and I for the forgiveness of sins, but he wanted to lead by example. He was fully divine but he was also fully human. By allowing himself to be baptized, Jesus demonstrated great love and respect for our humanity.

Each year the Church celebrates Jesus' baptism on the last day of the Christmas season. We celebrate his baptism because it reminds us of all Jesus did so that we could be reasonably happy in this life and happier than we can imagine with him forever in heaven.

Do you know when and where you were baptized? Baptism was the beginning of your new life in Jesus. This is when you became a member of his Church and joined the largest and most famous family in the world. You probably cannot remember your Baptism but it was one of the most powerful moments of your life.

Just as the Church celebrates Jesus' baptism, we should celebrate our own baptism. This year celebrate the day of your Baptism like you do your birthday.

First Reconciliation

Joseph was one of thirteen children. His older brothers disliked him very much because he had fabulous dreams. One day while he was working out in the fields, Joseph's brothers tricked him and sold him into slavery. He was sent to Egypt and forced to stay there, far from his family and friends.

A few years later, a terrible famine spread through the land and Joseph's family was starving. Egypt was the only country that had prepared for the famine, so the Pharaoh appointed a governor to be in charge of all the food. Joseph's brothers went to Egypt to beg the governor for food. They didn't realize that the governor was Joseph, the brother they had sold into slavery.

Joseph had a choice to make. He could either hold a grudge against his brothers for being so mean to him or he could choose to forgive them. What would you do? It wouldn't be easy to forgive them. He had suffered so much because of what his brothers had done to him, but Joseph was kind and merciful and chose to forgive them.

When Joseph revealed himself to his brothers they were amazed!

Life can be messy. We all make mistakes and from time to time we all do things that we know we shouldn't. We may not sell our siblings into slavery, but we do offend God and hurt others. We call this sin, and the thing about sin is that it makes us unhappy. Sin separates us from God, and we simply cannot be happy when we are separated from God. Reconciliation reunites us with God and fills us with joy again.

When did you receive your First Reconciliation? Your First Reconciliation was a great blessing and it is a blessing you can receive as many times as you wish for the rest of your life. I encourage you to go to Reconciliation and pour your heart out to God anytime you feel far from him. He will give you peace and courage to press on.

First Communion

Your journey with God is a great spiritual journey. Along the way you will have many decisions to make. Some will be big and some will be small. Every decision you make changes who you are forever. This is just one of the many reasons that God wants to help you become a fabulous decision maker.

You are preparing for your First Communion. Receiving Jesus in the Eucharist is one of the greatest blessings of our lives. But Holy Communion is not just a one time blessing. It is a lifelong blessing. Receiving Jesus in the Eucharist each and every Sunday at Mass will fill you with everything you need to live a fabulous life.

Jesus gives himself to you in the Eucharist. He gives you his encouragement so that you can persevere in times of difficulty. And he gives you his wisdom so you can become a great decision maker.

After your First Communion you will be able to receive Jesus in the Eucharist every Sunday for the rest of your life. In the Eucharist, Jesus wants to encourage you. He wants to help you persevere in times of difficulty, he wants to give you the wisdom you need to become a great decision maker, and he wants to teach you how to be a good friend to others.

One of the promises Jesus made to the disciples before he ascended into heaven was that he would always be with us. Jesus keeps this promise in the Eucharist. We go to church on Sunday to be with Jesus. In fact, anytime you are confused or upset or have some great news to share, it's great to stop by church and sit with Jesus for a few minutes. He waits for us in the tabernacle. It is a great blessing that Jesus will always be with us in the Eucharist.

Confirmation

God wants a dynamic collaboration with you. He doesn't just want to wave his hand and have everything happen exactly as he wants it to. God loves friendship and he wants to be your friend.

Before Jesus came to earth, an angel appeared to Mary and asked her if she would be willing to be mother to the Savior of the world. Mary said, "Yes!"

God didn't need Mary. He could have saved the world all by himself. But God didn't want it that way. God wanted a dynamic friendship with Mary.

God wants a dynamic friendship with you too.

But imagine what the world would be like if Mary didn't say yes? What would have happened if she said no to the mission God created her for?

God has created you for a special mission. There is a whole lot of need in the world. People are hungry and lonely and sick and scared. Your mission is to respond to some of that need. Your mission is going to ease the suffering of many. But, just like Mary, you have to choose whether or not you accept God's mission for your life.

Some people wonder why the world got to be such a mess. They wonder why is there so much pain and suffering in the world. The reason is simple: the world is a mess because lots of people said no to God and rejected their mission. When people say no to God and yes to selfishness, the world becomes a mess.

Just like Mary and the saints, you were made for mission. Say yes to God.

When you are a little older, you will receive the Sacrament of Confirmation. This is another amazing Sacrament. Through the Sacrament of Confirmation God will fill you with the Holy Spirit so that you can discover and fulfill the mission God has entrusted to you.

Marriage

God loves relationships, and he has a great desire for you to have fabulous relationships. One of the relationships he may choose to bless you with is marriage.

In the Sacrament of Marriage, God brings a man and a woman together to cherish each other, to love one another, and to help each other become the-best-version-of-themselves, grow in virtue, and live a holy life together.

If you go to a wedding, you might hear a passage read from St. Paul about love. His words have inspired every generation to love as God loves:

Love is patient and kind; love is not jealous or boastful; it is not arrogant or rude. Love does not insist on its own way; it is not irritable or resentful; it does not rejoice at wrong, but rejoices in the right. Love bears all things, believes all things, hopes all things, endures all things."

1 Corinthians 13:4—7

Holy Orders

Each Sunday the priest celebrates Mass. He blesses you, leads you in prayer, teaches you, sings with you, and nourishes your soul with the Body and Blood of Jesus.

But have you ever wondered what your priest does during the week?

Throughout the week, your priest visits the sick, prays for you and everyone in your parish, says Mass each day, buries the dead, spends time with the lonely, and encourages those in despair. But he does lots of ordinary things too, like exercise and eat, read and visit with family and friends.

Jesus laid his life down for us. He laid his life down for us on the cross, and he calls us all to lay down our lives for each other. A priest lays down his life to love God and serve God's people. It is the mission of the priest to love God by serving his people.

Since the time of Jesus, God has been choosing men to serve his people. In the Sacrament of Holy Orders, the Church ordains these men as deacons, priests, and bishops.

On the night before he died on the cross, Jesus washed the feet of his disciples. In Jesus' time only servants and slaves washed the feet of those in power. But Jesus was different. By example, Jesus showed that everyone is called to serve.

Anointing of the Sick

Every day miracles are dancing all around us. We read in the Gospels of Matthew, Mark, Luke, and John about Jesus' miracles: turning water into wine; healing the sick; making the blind see, the deaf hear, and the lame walk; casting out demons; feeding thousands; raising people from the dead; calming storms; and walking on water.

One day, four men carried their paralyzed friend on a mat to see Jesus. But when they arrived at the house where Jesus was teaching, they couldn't get inside. There were too many people.

The four men wanted so badly to help their friend that they went up on the roof and lowered him into the house before Jesus. Seeing the faith of these men, Jesus healed the paralyzed man, who immediately stood up and walked away.

You are on a great journey with God. If along the way you get sick and need God's healing for body, mind, or spirit, you will be blessed with the Anointing of the Sick.

Throughout your life, you will experience these great Catholic Moments we call Sacraments. Each of them is a blessing and they are all connected. These great Moments are designed by God to help you live a good life here on earth and prepare you to be blissfully happy with God forever in heaven.

You are blessed!

God Loves to Celebrate

We celebrate a lot as Catholics. We celebrate Easter and Christmas, we celebrate feast days and birthdays, we celebrate God, and we celebrate each other. Have you ever wondered why we celebrate so much as Catholics? The reason is because God loves to celebrate.

Favorite Days

Every day is special in its own way because life is special. Every day of life should be treasured. Life is precious. Life is sacred. Life is special.

Still, we all have favorites—favorite colors, favorite songs, and favorite foods. Do you have favorite days?

Some of my favorite days each year are Christmas, Easter, my birthday, and the feast days of my favorite saints. What are your three favorite days each year?

Your Special Day

God gives everyone a special day each year. We call this your birthday. What do you like to do on your birthday? What is your favorite birthday memory?

The First Time

Firsts matter. The first time you get to do anything is important. You never get that first time again.

Throughout the Gospels we often hear fabulous stories about the first time people met Jesus. One of the great examples of this is the story of Zacchaeus, a tax collector who was known for being a dishonest man.

One day when Jesus was walking, a huge crowd followed him, making it very difficult for anyone to see him. Zacchaeus wanted to see Jesus so badly that he climbed a tree just to catch a glimpse of him!

That first meeting with Jesus completely changed Zacchaeus' life. He renounced his dishonest ways and did his best to make up for all he had done wrong.

Firsts can be very special.

As we prepare for your First Communion, let's remember that you will never have this first again.

Every Sunday when you go to Mass you will be blessed to receive Jesus in the Eucharist. But there is something very special about the first time. So it is important for you to pay attention to everything that your parents and teachers are sharing with you about this very special event in your life.

You will never have this first again. Cherish it.

Feast Days

Catholics love to celebrate. So we have a whole year of celebrations planned. The high points of the Church's year are Christmas and Easter. But we also celebrate the great spiritual champions in our Catholic family. We call these men, women, and children saints!

Who is your favorite saint? When is his or her feast day? Why does this saint inspire you?

God's Favorite Day

God loves spending time with us. He loves it when we take a few minutes each day to talk to him. He loves it when we come to visit him at church on Sunday. He loves spending time with you. God smiles when he sees you at Mass on Sunday.

Sunday is God's favorite day.

What Makes Sunday Special?

Sunday is a special day.

Most people only get to enjoy about four thousand Sundays in their lives. Now, that may seem like a lot, but they go quickly. You have probably already experienced about 420 Sundays. So don't waste a single one. Make every Sunday a special day.

What are three ways you make Sunday a special day?
Go to church. Spend time with your family. Rest.

There are lots of special days, but most of them happen just
once a year, and some of them only happen once in your lifetime.
One of the beautiful things about Sunday is it happens every week.

Sunday is the Sabbath. The Sabbath is a special day of
rest and worship.

We all need to take a break from time to time to rest. Each night
we rest by sleeping. And once a week, God wants us to take a
special rest so that we can be filled with joy and share that joy
with everyone who comes into our lives.

The first story in the Bible is about God creating the world.
He finished creating on the sixth day, and the Bible tells us that he
rested on the seventh day. That's why we rest on Sunday. Rest is holy.

God loves you so much that he wants you to take good care of yourself.

We take care of ourselves by:

- Eating well
- Drinking plenty of water
- Exercising regularly
- Praying each day
- Getting enough sleep
- Resting on Sundays

Sunday is also a day of worship. We go to Mass to worship God. There are many ways to worship God, but one way we can do this every day is by thanking him for the many ways he has blessed us.

Have you counted your blessings today? What are you most grateful for today?

One of the things that make Sunday a special day is that we go to church. We praise and thank God by going to Mass each Sunday. What is the name of the church you go to for Mass on Sundays?

From the Bible: Creation

On the first day God created day and night, light and time.

On the second day God created the sky.

On the third day God created the earth, the seas, plants, and trees.

On the fourth day God created the sun, the moon, and the stars.

On the fifth day God created birds and fish.

On the sixth day God created cattle, insects, wild animals, and human beings.

And God didn't just create us; he created us in his image.

What does it mean that we are created in the image of God? It means God made us to resemble him. We can reason, we can dream, we know right from wrong, we are capable of holiness, and we thrive on healthy friendships.

To be made in the image of God is a great blessing, and blessings come with responsibility. God made humanity responsible stewards of all creation. He gave us the mind and the morality necessary to take care of all of creation.

When God had finished the work of creation, "he saw everything he had made, and indeed, it was very good" (Genesis 1:31).

God said—It is good! God blessed creation.

On the seventh day God rested. We call this the Sabbath, which means a day of rest and prayer.

Sunday is a day of rest. God blessed rest by resting himself.
By blessing rest he teaches us that rest is holy.

Sunday is also a day of gratitude.

One Sunday on the way to church, Max asked his dad, "Why do we
go to church every Sunday?" His dad smiled and replied, "Lots of
reasons. But one very important reason is to say thank you to God
for all the ways he has blessed us this week."

Every blessing comes from God!

Did you ever give someone a gift and he wasn't grateful? Perhaps he didn't say thank you, or maybe he tossed the gift aside as if it were a piece of junk. How did that make you feel?

God has blessed us with so many gifts. Going to Mass on Sunday is a great way to show God that we are grateful.

Listening to God at Mass

Have you ever wondered, "What is God really like?" It's a great question. We know many things about God and still he is a beautiful mystery because we do not know everything about him.

We know that God is love. We know God keeps his promises. We know that God cares about every single person. We know that God knows everything. We know that God is holy. We know that God is all-powerful. We know God has a plan. And we know that God is unchanging.

In the Bible we read about God speaking to Adam and Eve, Noah, Abraham, Moses, Isaac, Jacob, Rebekah, Mary, and many others.

Remember the last thing we said we know about God?
God is unchanging.

And just as he spoke to people in ancient times, he speaks to people in every time, and he speaks to you and me today.
He speaks to us through the Scriptures. He speaks to us through other people. He speaks to us through the Church. And he speaks to us in our hearts.

At Mass on Sunday God wants to speak to you. I like to bring a little journal with me to Mass to jot down the things he says to me in my heart.

I ask him at the beginning of Mass: "God, please show me one way in this Mass I can become a-better-version-of-myself this week." Then I listen to the readings, the prayers, the music, the homily, and the quiet of my heart, and write down the one thing that I sense God is saying to me.

Every Sunday at Mass, write the one thing God says to you in your Mass Journal. You will be amazed how God encourages you and challenges you to become the-best-version-of-yourself, grow in virtue, and live a holy life.

Every day is a new day in your journey with God—and every day God has a message he is trying to share with you.

Show What You Know

True or False

1. _____ You are on a journey toward your First Communion.

2. _____ You are blessed.

3. _____ God never likes to celebrate.

4. _____ You will only have one First Communion in your life.

5. _____ Sunday is a day for gratitude.

Fill in the blank

1. You are on a great _____ with God.

2. One of the greatest blessings you will ever receive
   in your life is the _____.

3. God is _____ you to a great banquet.

4. One way you can worship God every day
   is by counting your _____.

5. After God finished the work of creation, he said that
   everything was _____, even insects!

6. God created us in _____ image and likeness.

7. Sunday is a special day for _____

   and _____.

8. We _____ and _____ God by
   going to Mass each Sunday.

9. Just as he did in ancient times, God _____ to
   you and me.

10. Going to Mass on Sunday is a great way to show God we are
    _____.

Word Bank

PRAISE	SPEAKS	JOURNEY	GOOD	THANK	INVITING	REST	HIS
	GRATEFUL	EUCHARIST	WORSHIP	BLESSINGS			

Journal with Jesus

Dear Jesus,

Sundays are special because . . .

_____

_____

_____

_____

_____

_____

_____

_____

Closing Prayer

When Zechariah's son, John the Baptist, was born, he was overwhelmed with gratitude. After months of not being able to speak, Zechariah burst into a song of praise, thanking God for all the incredible gifts he had been given.

Zechariah reminds us of the importance of voicing our gratitude to God.

Jesus is with us always in the Eucharist. This is an incredible gift! To show God how grateful we are for the gift of Jesus, let's praise him using the words of Zechariah:

Blessed be the Lord,
The God of Israel;
He has come to his people and set them free.

He has raised up for us a mighty Savior,
Born of the house of his servant David.

Through his holy prophets he promised of old
That he would save us from our enemies,
From the hands of all who hate us.

He promised to show mercy to our fathers
And to remember his holy Covenant.

This was the oath he swore to our father Abraham:
To set us free from the hands of our enemies,
Free to worship him without fear,
Holy and righteous in his sight
All the days of our life.

From Luke 1:68–75

2

The Greatest Event on Earth

God, our loving Father,
thank you for all the ways you bless me.
Help me to be aware that every person,
place, and adventure I experience is an
opportunity to love you more.
Fill me with a desire to change and to grow,
and give me the grace to become
the-best-version-of-myself in
every moment of every day.

Amen.

The Ultimate Prayer

You are blessed. One of the greatest blessings God gives us as Catholics is the Mass.

There are many different types of prayer. There are prayers of thanksgiving, in which we thank God for all the ways he blesses us. There are prayers of petition or intercession, in which we ask God for some favor. There are prayers of praise, in which we praise God for being God. And there are prayers of adoration, in which we adore God.

One of the incredible things about the Mass is that it combines all these forms of prayer. This is just one of the many reasons why the Mass is the ultimate prayer. Another reason is because in it we present a perfect offering to God. Jesus, who died for us on the cross, is that perfect offering.

Each time you receive Jesus in Holy Communion, God will fill you up in a special way with his grace so that you can become the-best-version-of-yourself!

It is a great privilege to go to Mass each Sunday. The Mass is the ultimate prayer. It is the perfect way for us to gather together as a community of believers and praise God.

At Mass we remember Jesus' last meal, his death on the cross, and his Resurrection. We also get to receive him in the Eucharist. The Eucharist is a celebration of God's love for us and a reminder that God is always with us.

Your First Communion is going to be a very special day in your life.

God's House

Where do we celebrate Mass? At God's house! That's right. The church is God's house. God is so brilliant that he knew in his almighty wisdom that it would be important for us to spend time with him at his house.

Why? Well, have you ever noticed that when you are around people who are good, kind, generous, and thoughtful, you get inspired to be good, kind, generous, and thoughtful too?

When we spend time with God he inspires us to be good— and not just good, but our best. God wants you to live the best life imaginable and he wants you to become the-best-version-of-yourself, grow in virtue, and live a holy life.

When we spend time with God, he fills us with his grace so that we can live holy lives. So each Sunday he invites us over to his house for a great celebration. We call that celebration the Mass. But God is always happy to see us. Sometimes it is nice just to stop by church in the middle of the week and sit in the pews and talk to God about whatever is happening in your life. He loves it when we talk to him about what is happening in our lives.

The Third Commandment

When Moses went to the top of Mount Sinai to speak with God, God didn't give him one hundred commandments or a thousand commandments. How many commandments did God give Moses to share with the people?

That's right. Just ten.

Do you remember what we said about the Ten Commandments when we were preparing for your First Reconciliation? Let's take another look.

The Ten Commandments are a blessing from God given to his people. They help us become the-best-version-of-ourselves, grow in virtue, and live holy lives. They show us the best way to live.

And because there are so few, every single one is very important.

Do you remember what the third commandment is?
That's right. "Remember to keep holy the Lord's Day."

Sunday is the Lord's Day. It is the Sabbath. It is God's day. And this is really important to remember. How do we keep the Sabbath holy? By going to Mass.

Going to Mass is the most important thing on Sunday. God wants to see us and spend time with us. Even if we have a soccer game or a camping trip, God still expects us to plan a time to go to Mass.

He gives you life every moment of every day. He fills your life with fabulous opportunities. He blesses you in so many ways. And he asks that you visit him for one hour each week.

How many hours are there in a week? There are seven days in a week, and twenty-four hours in a day: 7 x 24 = 168. Out of 168 hours each week, God asks that you come to his house for one hour. Is that too much to ask?

We should be excited to get there each Sunday to thank God for all the ways he has blessed us, to thank him for life, and just to spend time with him.

Listening to God

When you get to church each Sunday it is good to take a few minutes to get quiet before Mass begins. This helps us to hear what God wants to say to us.

God speaks to us in so many ways.

God speaks to us through the Bible. He speaks to us through the Church. He speaks to us in our hearts. He speaks to us through other people and through situations. And he speaks to our hearts in a special way at Mass.

Learning to listen to God's voice is one of the most important lessons we can learn in life. But learning to hear his voice clearly takes a lot of practice. One great way to practice is at Mass on Sunday. In some ways, we come to Mass on Sunday to get our instructions for the week from God.

You probably won't hear an actual voice when God speaks to you. He might speak to you through one of the readings, or through the music or homily, or he may just speak to you in the quiet of your heart.

God might say, "I want you to practice being more patient with your little brother this week." He might say, "I want you to listen to your parents and do what they ask you to do without hesitation." Or he might say, "I want you to enjoy nature while you are on your vacation this week."

God has a special message for us every week. That's why it's important to go to Mass every Sunday. Without God's instructions and directions, we get lost.

Every Sunday at church God has something he wants to tell you. It's unique every week. That's why he invites you to come to Mass every Sunday, so you can hear the special thing he wants to say to you.

Last time you were at church, what did God say to you? Do you remember? Were you listening?

Your Mass Journal

Do you ever feel like God is trying to tell you something? God is always trying to speak to us, but learning to listen to God in the many ways he speaks to us takes time and practice.

When God spoke to Jonah, he told Jonah about a very special mission he had planned for him. Well, Jonah didn't like what God was asking him to do, so instead of listening to God, Jonah tried to run away.

But God didn't give up on Jonah. Instead, God sent a giant whale to swallow Jonah whole! For three days and three nights Jonah lived in the belly of the whale. Once Jonah finally started listening to God, God rescued Jonah from the whale and sent him off to fulfill his mission.

God has always spoken to his people. And he wants to speak to you too.

Next Sunday, take a little notebook to Mass with you. This will be your Mass Journal. Listen to the music, listen to the readings, listen to the prayers, listen to the homily, and listen to your heart. Before Mass begins, pray, "Dear God, please show me one way in this Mass that I can become a-better-version-of-myself this week."

Then listen, wait patiently, and when you sense the one thing that God is saying to you, write it down. Pray for the rest of the Mass about how you can live that one thing this week, and ask God to help you.

There are many wonderful reasons why we go to Mass on Sunday, and one of them is to listen to God's voice.

From the Bible: The Road to Emmaus

A few days after Jesus rose from the dead, two of his disciples were walking from Jerusalem to a village called Emmaus. They were talking about Jesus and all the incredible things that had happened. While they were talking Jesus came up beside them, but their eyes were kept from recognizing him. He said to them, "What are you talking about?"

They stopped and looked at him. Then one of them said, "Are you the only person in Jerusalem who does not know the things that have taken place there the past few days?"

"What things?" he asked them.

"The things about Jesus of Nazareth, a great and wise teacher, who died and has now risen from the dead."

Then Jesus spoke to them about how it was necessary for the Messiah to suffer before entering into his glory, and he explained all the places in the Scriptures that referred to him.

As they approached Emmaus they invited him to join them for a meal. So he went in to stay with them. When he was at table with them, he took bread, blessed and broke it, and gave it to them. Then their eyes were opened and they recognized him, and he vanished.

They said to each other, "Were not our hearts burning within us as he spoke to us along the road?"

Amazed, they got up and returned to Jerusalem to tell the others, "We have seen the Lord; he is indeed risen."

Adapted from Luke 24:13–35

The risen Jesus is always at our side, but often we don't recognize him. Jesus is by our side when we wake up each morning, he is by our side when we are playing with friends, he is by our side when we are at baseball and ballet, he is by our side when we are doing our homework, he is by our side when we go shopping, and he is by our side when we go to bed at night.

In the morning, he is so excited for you to wake up and start a new day. At soccer he is cheering for you to do your best. And when you go shopping, he is whispering in your ear, "Is what you are about to buy going to help you become the-best-version-of-yourself?"

Jesus is present in a special way at Mass. The disciples had a powerful encounter with Jesus on the road to Emmaus, but you get to have an even more powerful encounter with him each Sunday at Mass. And very soon you are going to be able to receive Jesus in the Eucharist.

So Many Wonders

There are so many wonderful things that happen during the Mass. If you went to Mass every day of your life, you would still be discovering its wonders at the end of your life. There is nothing like the Mass.

We have already talked about how God speaks to us at Mass. That is amazing. The Eucharist is another wonder we experience at Mass. We believe that during the Mass, a simple piece of bread and a cup of wine are transformed into the Body and Blood of Jesus. That is amazing!

It is amazing that God gives himself to us in this way. At Mass God gives himself to us completely in the Eucharist, and at Mass we give ourselves completely to him in prayer. We are going to talk a lot more about this in the coming pages.

Sometimes people say they are bored at Mass. Usually this is because they don't know what is going on or because they are not listening to what God is saying to them. It is impossible to be bored at Mass if we are trying to listen to God's voice. If we ever find Mass boring, it's time for us to put more energy into our conversation with God.

If we find Mass uninteresting, perhaps we need to learn more about what is actually happening. Everything that happens at Mass happens for a reason, and when we really know what is going on, it is fascinating.

Sometimes it helps to have a missal, a small book that explains everything that is happening in the Mass. It can be very helpful to follow along.

Another way to make sure we don't get bored at Mass is to sing all the songs and respond to all the prayers. When you participate in Mass you are in a conversation with God. It is only when we stop participating that we get bored. Plus, when we talk with God, he tells us amazing things!

As we grow in wisdom we discover that the Mass is the most amazing event on earth!

Show What You Know

True or False

1. _____ Your First Communion is going to be a very special day in your life.

2. _____ God wants you to live the worst life imaginable.

3. _____ The Ten Commandments show us the best way to live.

4. _____ God never speaks to us.

5. _____ Every Sunday at church God has something he wants to tell you.

Fill in the blank

1. Each Sunday God invites us over to his _____ for a great celebration.

2. The _____ is one of the greatest blessings God gives us as Catholics.

3. The Eucharist is a _____ of God's love for us.

4. When we spend time with God he fills us with _____ so that we can live holy lives.

5. The Ten Commandments are a _____ God gives us to help us become the-best-version-of-ourselves.

6. It is _____ to be bored at Mass if we are trying to listen to God's voice.

7. The Mass is the _____ prayer.

8. Learning to _____ to God's voice is one of the most important lessons we can learn in life.

9. If you went to Mass every day of your life, you would still be discovering its _____ at the end of your life.

10. As you grow in wisdom you discover that the Mass is the most _____ event on earth.

Word Bank

HOUSE	AMAZING	CELEBRATION	IMPOSSIBLE	GRACE
MASS	ULTIMATE	LISTEN	WONDERS	BLESSING

Journal with Jesus

Dear Jesus,

I am excited to receive you in the Eucharist for the first time because . . .

_____

_____

_____

_____

_____

_____

_____

Closing Prayer

Tragically, there are many people who spend their whole lives not knowing Jesus and how much he loves them. This is very sad.

The reason they never meet Jesus is because they never go looking for him. God speaks to us in many ways. He speaks to us through the Church, the Bible, the Mass, nature, great art and literature, and one another. But to hear God, to meet him, to discover his amazing plan for your life, you need to seek him!

Let's pray together now and ask God to give us the courage and the desire to always seek him, no matter what:

> **Be, Lord Jesus,**
> **a bright flame before me,**
> **a guiding star above me,**
> **a smooth path below me,**
> **a kindly shepherd behind me:**
> **today, tonight, and forever.**
>
> **Amen.**

Prayer of St. Columba

3

The Word of God

God, our loving Father,
thank you for all the ways you bless me.
Help me to be aware that every person,
place, and adventure I experience is an
opportunity to love you more.
Fill me with a desire to change and to grow,
and give me the grace to become
the-best-version-of-myself in
every moment of every day.

Amen.

Overview of the Mass

Each time you go to Mass there are many things that happen. Behind each prayer and each action is enormous meaning; everything in the Mass happens for a reason. In our spiritual journey as Catholics we are always uncovering new layers of meaning, so we never stop learning about the Mass.

The Mass is made up of four parts:

1. **The Introductory Rites**

2. **The Liturgy of the Word**

3. **The Liturgy of the Eucharist**

4. **The Concluding Rites**

There are two words for us to pay special attention to here: rite and liturgy.

What Is a Rite?

A rite is something that is said or done the same way every time for a reason. For example, the Sign of the Cross is a rite. We do it the same way every time. We say it the same way every time: "In the name of the Father, and of the Son, and of the Holy Spirit. Amen."

The order is for a reason. God the Father is the first person of the Blessed Trinity. God the Son is the second person of the Holy Trinity. And God the Holy Spirit is the third person of the Holy Trinity.

If you went to Mass and the priest began by making the Sign of the Cross and saying, "In the name of the Son, and of the Holy Spirit, and of the Father. Amen," you would know that something was wrong.

Our Catholic faith has many rites.
Each rite has a reason.

What Is Liturgy?

Liturgy is a prayer we participate in as a community. During the Mass we experience two types of liturgy: the Liturgy of the Word and the Liturgy of the Eucharist.

During the Liturgy of the Word we listen to readings from the Bible and a homily from the priest or deacon, then we pray the Creed together and offer our petitions to God.

During the Liturgy of the Eucharist we offer our lives and our gifts to God, prepare the altar, pray the Eucharistic Prayer, and receive Holy Communion.

Liturgy is a beautiful way to spend time with God and our parish family.

Where Do We Celebrate Mass?

We celebrate Mass at church. Our parish church is a very special place because it is God's house. We gather at church with our family, friends, and all our parish family to worship God in the way that Jesus taught us to.

The Mass is a beautiful ritual made up of prayers, liturgies, and rites. During the Mass we use many special items to help us celebrate. Do you recognize any of these items?

The Introductory Rites

We come to church on Sunday to celebrate Mass. It's a great way to thank God for all the blessings he has given us.

During the Mass we remember Jesus' life, death, and Resurrection, and the most amazing thing happens, something that doesn't happen anywhere else: the priest changes bread and wine into the Body and Blood of Jesus.

How can he do this? God gives priests special powers. At your First Reconciliation God forgave your sins through the priest. During Mass God transforms the bread and wine into the Body and Blood of Jesus through the priest.

Another amazing thing that happens at church is that we get to receive Holy Communion. We get to receive Jesus in the Eucharist. This is an amazing blessing.

When you go back to your pew after you receive Jesus in the Eucharist, kneel down, close your eyes, and pray. This is a very special moment because God is inside you.

Now let's talk about the four parts of the Mass. Do you remember what they are?

1. **The Introductory Rites**

2. **The Liturgy of the Word**

3. **The Liturgy of the Eucharist**

4. **The Concluding Rites**

The Introductory Rites

Mass begins with this procession. The priest, deacon, readers, and altar servers walk together in procession toward the altar. This procession is usually accompanied by music. Music helps us to raise our hearts to God in praise and thanksgiving.

Have you ever noticed that music can make you very joyful? This is your heart and soul leaping for joy. Music is a powerful way to pray. Saint Augustine said, "Singing is like praying twice."

Once the priest gets to the altar he begins with the Sign of the Cross: "In the name of the Father, and of the Son, and of the Holy Spirit. Amen."

The Sign of the Cross is a rite.

We Say Sorry

God loves healthy relationships, and a very important part of healthy relationships is saying sorry when we do or say something that hurts the other person. Catholics say sorry. The reason is because our friendship with God and our friendships with each other cannot thrive if we don't say sorry.

If you were playing on the playground with a friend yesterday and he pushed you over and didn't say sorry, how would you feel? You might wonder if he was really your friend. But if he came up to you and the first thing he did was say, "I'm sorry I pushed you over yesterday. I won't do it again. Please forgive me."

How would that make you feel? You would be reminded that he really does want to be your friend.

That's why, after the Sign of the Cross, the first thing we do at Mass is say sorry to God. We want him to know that we are his friends and that we want to be really good friends to him.

We say sorry to God and ask for forgiveness at the beginning of Mass with a really simple and beautiful prayer:

> **Priest: Lord Have Mercy**
> **Congregation: Lord Have Mercy**
> **Priest: Christ Have Mercy**
> **Congregation: Christ Have Mercy**
> **Priest: Lord Have Mercy**
> **Congregation: Lord Have Mercy**

Glory to God

Next we say or sing The Gloria.

At different times in life we pray for different reasons.
And at different times in the Mass we pray for different reasons.

Sometimes we pray to ask God to help us. This is called a prayer
of petition. Sometimes we pray to ask God to help other people.
This is called a prayer of intercession. Sometimes we pray to thank
God for all the ways he has blessed us. This is called a prayer
of thanksgiving. And sometimes we pray to praise God for his
goodness. This is called a prayer of praise.

The Gloria is a prayer of praise. Sometimes we sing it and
sometimes we say it, but always for the same reason
—to praise God!

Glory to God in the highest,

and on earth peace to people of good will.

We praise you, we bless you, we adore you, we glorify you.

We give you thanks for your great glory,

Lord God, heavenly King,

O God, almighty Father.

Lord Jesus Christ, Only Begotten Son, Lord God,

Lamb of God, Son of the Father,

You take away the sins of the world, have mercy on us;

You take away the sins of the world, receive our prayer;

You are seated at the right hand of the Father, have mercy on us.

For you alone are the Holy One,

You alone are the Lord,

You alone are the Most High, Jesus Christ,

With the Holy Spirit, in the glory of God the Father. Amen.

After the Gloria, the priest reads the opening prayer from the Roman Missal. Then the whole congregation responds with "Amen," and we sit down to listen to the Word of God.

The Liturgy of the Word

During the part of the Mass we call the Liturgy of the Word, we listen to the Word of God and reflect on how we can live our lives as God invites us to.

The Liturgy of the Word includes readings from the Bible, the homily, the Creed, and the intercessory prayers.

At Mass on Sunday we listen to four readings from the Bible:

1. **The First Reading, from the Old Testament**

2. **The Responsorial Psalm**

3. **The Second Reading, from the New Testament**

4. **The Gospel Reading, from one of the four Gospels: Matthew, Mark, Luke, and John**

Each reading is specifically selected to connect with a theme that the Church wants us to reflect on that week. And guess what: Every Catholic parish reads the same readings each Sunday.

So if you have a friend on the other side of the country, you can talk about the readings because they heard the same ones you heard at Mass.

Different people read different readings. Perhaps one day you will become a reader at Mass. There are so many ways to be involved in the life of the parish—reading at Mass is just one of them.

You are a layperson. A layperson is an unordained member of the Church, and he or she usually reads the First Reading, the Responsorial Psalm, and the Second Reading. The priest or the deacon reads the Gospel. Both the priest and deacon are ordained members of the Church.

Some parishes don't have Mass every Sunday because there are not enough priests. This is very sad. Some Sundays these parishes have to have Eucharistic services instead of Mass. During a Eucharistic service we still listen to the readings of the Mass and the Eucharist is distributed from the tabernacle. In this case a layperson can read the Gospel.

After the Gospel, the priest or deacon delivers the homily. During the homily, the priest or deacon explains the readings, shows us how they apply to our lives, and inspires us to live what we have just heard from God's Word.

93

We Believe

After the homily, we stand and proclaim the Creed together, and then we have the prayers of the faithful.

Everyone believes something. There are many things we believe as Catholics. We believe in God, we believe God loves us, we believe God has blessed us, and we believe in the power of prayer. But there are many other things we believe.

At Mass each Sunday we proclaim the Creed. The Creed is a summary of the core beliefs that make up our Catholic faith.

The Creed

I BELIEVE IN ONE GOD, **THE FATHER ALMIGHTY,**

maker of heaven and earth

OF ALL THINGS VISIBLE AND INVISIBLE.

I BELIEVE IN ONE LORD JESUS CHRIST,

THE ONLY BEGOTTEN SON OF GOD, BORN OF THE FATHER BEFORE ALL AGES.

GOD FROM GOD, *Light from Light,*

TRUE GOD FROM TRUE GOD,

BEGOTTEN, NOT MADE, CONSUBSTANTIAL WITH THE FATHER;

THROUGH HIM ALL THINGS WERE MADE.

FOR US MEN AND FOR OUR SALVATION *he came down from heaven,*

AND BY THE HOLY SPIRIT

was incarnate of the Virgin Mary

AND BECAME MAN.

FOR OUR SAKE HE WAS CRUCIFIED UNDER PONTIUS PILATE,

HE SUFFERED DEATH AND WAS BURIED,

and rose again on the third day

IN ACCORDANCE WITH THE SCRIPTURES.

HE ASCENDED INTO HEAVEN

AND IS SEATED AT THE RIGHT HAND OF THE FATHER.

HE WILL COME AGAIN IN GLORY

to judge the living and the dead

AND HIS KINGDOM WILL HAVE NO END.

I believe in the Holy Spirit, the Lord, the giver of life,

WHO PROCEEDS FROM THE FATHER AND THE SON,

WHO WITH THE FATHER AND THE SON IS ADORED AND GLORIFIED,

who has spoken through the prophets.

I BELIEVE IN ONE, HOLY, CATHOLIC AND APOSTOLIC CHURCH.

I CONFESS ONE BAPTISM FOR THE FORGIVENESS OF SINS

and I look forward to the resurrection of the dead

AND THE LIFE OF THE WORLD TO COME.

Amen.

From the Bible: The Sower of Seeds

As Jesus made his way from village to village, word about his great deeds spread very quickly. He became very famous as a great teacher and healer, and so everywhere he went huge crowds of people would gather around him.

One day Jesus was sitting by the lake, and a large crowd gathered around him. They wanted him to teach them and heal them. So Jesus sat in a boat at the water's edge, the people stood around, and he told them parables. One of those parables was about a farmer sowing seeds.

A farmer went out to sow seeds in his field. As he sowed the seeds, some fell on the path beside the field, and birds came down and ate them. Other seeds fell on rocky ground, where there was not sufficient soil. These seeds sprang up quickly, but because of the shallow soil, when the sun rose it scorched them and they died. Still other seeds fell among thorns, and as they grew they were choked by the thorns. But some seeds fell on the rich, good soil, and these grew strong and healthy, and brought forth an abundant harvest.

God is the farmer. Our hearts and souls are the soil. The world, selfishness, and evil are the birds, the thorns, and the scorching hot sun. Daily prayer, learning about our faith, going to Mass on Sunday, being generous to all who cross our path, and sharing God's message with others all help to make your heart and soul like the rich soil that receives the seed and produces an abundant harvest.

Adapted from Matthew 13:1–9

Wear It Out

All of the readings at Mass come from the most famous book in the world: the Bible. It is the best-selling book of all time. When you pick up the Bible it may seem like you are holding one big book, but in fact, it is a collection of 73 books.

The Bible is made up of two main sections: the Old Testament and the New Testament. There are 46 books in the Old Testament and 27 books in the New Testament.

One of the many ways God speaks to us is through the Bible. God has an amazing plan for your life, and one of the ways he reveals that amazing plan is through the readings we hear at Mass every Sunday.

If you were going on a long journey it would be a good idea to take a map with you. It would be even better to take a guide with you who has made the journey before. The Bible is like that map and the Church is like that guide to help you make your journey through this life into the next so that you can live with God in heaven forever.

Over and over throughout the Bible God speaks to people, guiding them, encouraging them, and warning them. He spoke to Adam and Eve, Moses and Abraham, Noah and Jacob, Rebecca and Ruth, Mary and Paul. God spoke to each of them in different ways, but he spoke to them all. And now, God wants to speak to you.

Jesus is the central figure in the Bible. In the Old Testament we read over and over again about how the people were waiting for Jesus, the Messiah, to come. The New Testament is about Jesus and his teachings and about the life of the early Church and how the first Christians tried to live the Gospel message.

I have had some wonderful teachers in my life, and I am sure you have too. Jesus is the greatest teacher who ever lived. His favorite way to teach was to tell stories. He told stories that ordinary people could understand.

Do you have a favorite Bible story?

Do you have a favorite shirt or sweater? Do you have a favorite pair of shoes? I have an old sweatshirt that I just love. It is all worn out. The color is fading and there are a couple of holes in it, but it is so comfortable. It has been with me in good times and in bad times, and it comforts me in ways that a new sweatshirt cannot.

Many years ago a good friend inspired and challenged me. He said, "One of my goals in life is to wear out a Bible." I thought to myself, "What a fabulous goal."

Now I want to challenge you. Get yourself a Bible to carry with you throughout your life. Ask your parents or grandparents to read a little to you each day. As you get older, read a little yourself each day. Wear that Bible out by reading it, reflecting on what you learn, and praying for the grace to live what you learn.

Over a lifetime Jesus and the other great people in the Bible will become great friends of yours. They will teach you how to grow in virtue, become the-best-version-of-yourself, and live a holy life.

Somewhere down the road, I hope we meet, and when we do, I hope you will show me your worn-out Bible.

God wants you to have many companions on your journey to heaven. He wants you to have friends who help you become the-best-version-of-yourself. But he also wants you to be friends with the saints because they have already made this journey and can teach you so much about which path to take and the paths to avoid. God also gives us our guardian angels to accompany us on the journey. And God gives us the Bible and the Church as great companions along the way too.

Show What You Know

True or False

1. _____ The Bible is a great companion for your journey to heaven.

2. _____ We should never say sorry even when we've done something wrong.

3. _____ There is no purpose or meaning behind each prayer and each action at Mass.

4. _____ God speaks to you through the Bible.

5. _____ Jesus is the greatest teacher who ever lived.

Fill in the blank

1. God has an amazing _____ for your life.

2. Our parish church is a very special place because it is God's _____.

3. God reveals his amazing plan for your life through the _____ you hear at Mass every Sunday.

4. Going to Mass on Sunday is a great way to thank God for all the _____ he has given you.

5. At Mass we get to receive _____ in the Eucharist.

6. Music helps us to raise our hearts to God in _____ and _____.

7. God loves _____ relationships.

8. The _____ is the most famous book in the world.

9. One of the many ways God _____ to you is through the Bible.

10. The Bible is your _____ and the Church is your _____ on your journey to live with God in heaven forever.

Word Bank

THANKSGIVING	HOUSE	GUIDE	HEALTHY	SPEAKS	PRAISE	PLAN
READINGS	MAP	BIBLE	JESUS	BLESSINGS		

Journal with Jesus

Dear Jesus,

You are the greatest teacher in history; I need your help understanding . . .

_____

_____

_____

_____

_____

_____

_____

_____

Closing Prayer

Throughout your life, you will come across many teachers. But none of them will ever love you more or possess greater wisdom than Jesus.

From time to time you will really want to become the-best-version-of-yourself, grow in virtue, and live a holy life but you won't know how to do it. Those are the moments when you go to Jesus, the greatest teacher who ever lived, and ask him for help.

St. Ignatius of Loyola was a great priest and teacher. He founded one of the largest and most influential religious orders in history, the Society of Jesus (better known as the Jesuits). He was a spiritual master because he knew how to ask Jesus for help.

Together let's use the words of St. Ignatius and ask God to teach us to become all he created us to be:

Lord, teach me to be generous. Teach me to serve you as you deserve; to give and not to count the cost, to fight and not to heed the wounds, to toil and not to seek for rest, to labor and not to ask for reward, save that of knowing that I do your will.

Amen.

4

The Eucharist

God, our loving Father,
thank you for all the ways you bless me.
Help me to be aware that every person,
place, and adventure I experience is an
opportunity to love you more.
Fill me with a desire to change and to grow,
and give me the grace to become
the-best-version-of-myself in
every moment of every day.

Amen.

Food for the Soul

God has blessed you in so many ways, but he isn't finished blessing you. There are still thousands of blessings God wants to shower upon you. One of the great blessings God wants to share with you is the Eucharist. Every day you are getting closer to receiving Jesus in the Eucharist! Are you excited?

The Eucharist is food for the soul. That's right, your soul gets hungry just like your body gets hungry. It's easy to tell when your body gets hungry because your tummy growls and you feel weak and tired. But how do you know when your soul is hungry? When our souls are hungry we become restless, impatient, angry, and selfish. But most of all, we find it harder to do what we know we should do.

When our souls get hungry we need to feed them. The Eucharist is the ultimate soul food, but we can also feed our souls with prayer, the Scriptures, and serving other people.

You feed your body every day. You don't wait until it is starving before you feed it. You have a regular routine of meals and snacks to make sure your body has the food and energy it needs to thrive. We need a routine like that for feeding our souls too. This routine includes daily prayer, grace before meals, service to others, and of course, Sunday Mass.

The Mass is an incredible blessing because it feeds your soul in many ways. The Word of God feeds your soul, receiving the Body and Blood of Jesus in the Eucharist feeds your soul, and participating in a community of faith feeds your soul.

We've already talked about the Word of God and how important it is to listen to God. Now let's talk about how he feeds us with the Eucharist.

The Liturgy of the Eucharist

You are so blessed to be Catholic. One of the many reasons you are blessed to be Catholic is the Eucharist. You get to receive the Body and Blood of Jesus. The Eucharist is uniquely Catholic.

You are Catholic. You are blessed.

The Liturgy of the Eucharist is broken up into three parts: the Offering, the Eucharistic Prayer, and the reception of Holy Communion.

This is all very important, so let's go over it together, step by step.

The Offertory

Throughout the Mass, God gives us moments to pause and experience its many wonders. The offertory is one of those moments.

During the offertory a family from the parish usually brings the bread and wine, along with the money we put in the collection for the Church and the poor. Then the priest prepares the gifts to offer them to God.

As the gifts are being brought forward and the priest is preparing the gifts, we offer ourselves completely to God. We can do this with a simple prayer in our hearts. Here is an example:

> **Lord, I give myself completely to you right now. Teach me, lead me, and feed me with the Eucharist so I can serve you powerfully here in this world and live with you forever in heaven.**

The offertory is also a great time to bring our problems to God and ask for his help. If there is someone you know who is suffering or something that you are struggling with, ask Jesus to heal the situation. He is the great healer. The offertory is a perfect time to ask Jesus the Healer to intervene in your life. Here are some examples:

> **Jesus, help me study hard for my test.**
> **Jesus, my friend is sick. Help her to get better.**
> **Jesus, my brother hurt my feelings. Help me to forgive him.**
> **Jesus, help me to listen better to my parents.**

You are on a great journey with God. Your destination is heaven. God wants to be your guide and companion on this journey. He wants to be invited into every detail of your life so that he can best guide and advise you. He wants to show you the best way to live. God wants to help you become the-best-version-of-yourself, grow in virtue, and live a holy life.

The Eucharistic Prayer

We've always celebrated the presence of God.

The Jewish people believed that God was present in the Ark of the Covenant. For a long time, the Ark was lost. This was a very sad time for the Jewish people. They tried very hard to find it because they wanted to be close to God.

When King David brought the Ark of the Covenant to Jerusalem, the people were overjoyed. So was King David. He was so happy that when he brought the Ark back to his people, he danced with great joy. Nothing made King David happier than being in the presence of God.

The Eucharist is God in our midst.

Every time we go to Mass or visit a Catholic Church where Jesus is inside the tabernacle, God is physically with us in the Eucharist. The word Eucharist means "thanksgiving:" we are thankful to have God with us always.

The Eucharistic Prayer is the most important part of the Mass because this is when Jesus comes to be with us. This is when the bread and wine become the Body and Blood of Jesus.

During the Eucharistic Prayer we thank God for his friendship and for coming once again through the Eucharist to share his life with us.

The Consecration

The consecration is the moment when the bread and wine become the Body and Blood of Jesus. This is an incredible moment—that's why we kneel down for the consecration. Kneeling is a simple and profound sign of reverence. When we kneel during the Mass, it is a sign that something amazing is about to happen.

Just before kneeling, we pray the *Holy, Holy, Holy* together as a parish family:

Holy, Holy, Holy Lord God of Hosts.
Heaven and earth are full of your glory.
Hosanna in the highest.
Blessed is he who comes in the name of the Lord.
Hosanna in the highest.

Now we kneel and prepare for the great moment of consecration. Leading up to the consecration, the priest reminds us what happened at the Last Supper, the very first Eucharist.

To consecrate the bread and the wine, the priest says the same words Jesus said during the Last Supper:

This is my Body, which is given up for you;
This is the Blood of the new and everlasting covenant,
do this in memory of me.

Our Father

This is the moment of consecration. After the priest says these words, the bread and wine become the Body and Blood of Jesus. The consecration of the Eucharist is one of the great mysteries of our faith.

The Eucharistic Prayer ends with the Great Amen. Sometimes we say the Amen and sometimes we sing it. Either way we should say it loud and with confidence. This is our way of saying, "Yes! Jesus, I believe in you! I believe that the bread and the wine just became your Body and Blood!"

Following the Great Amen, we stand and pray the *Our Father* together.

Do you remember one of the main reasons why Jesus taught us this prayer? We talked about it while preparing for your First Reconciliation. Let's revisit it for a moment.

You are blessed. You are the son or daughter of a great King. Jesus wanted us to always remember that God is our Father and that we are children of God.

The *Our Father* reminds us of the first blessing God gives us: life!

After the *Our Father*, the priest asks God to fill us with his peace. Remember how earlier we talked about your soul getting hungry? One sign that your soul is hungry is that you don't have peace in your heart. Your soul craves peace.

God wants to fill you with his peace so that you can go out into the world and share it with everyone who crosses your path.

Holy Communion

When you receive Holy Communion Jesus gives himself completely to you. In the prayers leading up to the consecration we remember that Jesus died for us on the cross to save us from our sins. This is not meant to make you feel guilty; it is meant to make you feel loved. God wants you to remember how much you mean to him.

One of the most famous passages in the entire Bible is John 3:16:

**For God so loved the world that he sent his only Son,
so that everyone who believes in him may not perish
but have eternal life.**

God loved you so much that he sent his son, Jesus, so that you could have eternal life. For God so loved YOU that he sent Jesus so that YOU may have eternal life! You are loved and indeed blessed!

Let's say this out loud together:

God loves me so much that he sent his son Jesus so that I could have eternal life and live with him forever in heaven.

How did that feel?

God always wants you to feel loved. And when we receive Jesus in the Eucharist this is a special moment of God's love.

If you ever get to climb a huge mountain, the feeling of looking out across the vast surroundings from the top of that mountain is an amazing experience. The Mass is like climbing a great mountain. Receiving the Eucharist is the top of the mountain, the pinnacle of the Mass.

God feeds us the ultimate food for the soul at the mountaintop of the Mass. The Eucharist is food for the soul. Every Sunday at Mass God fills us with the Eucharist to become the-best-version-of-ourselves, grow in virtue, and live holy lives.

Receiving Holy Communion is an incredible gift that we should never take for granted.

When the moment arrives to receive Jesus, you will stand before the priest, deacon, or extraordinary minister and he will raise the host and say, "The Body of Christ." You will respond by saying, "Amen," and then consume the Host.

The True Presence

Jesus is truly present in the Eucharist. It is not a symbol; it is Jesus. This is one of the most beautiful mysteries of the Catholic faith.

When Jesus first started telling people about the Eucharist, some found it difficult to believe. Throughout the centuries, others have had doubts about Jesus being truly present in the Eucharist too.

In the 8th century there was a priest in Italy who was having these doubts. One day while he was saying Mass, as he consecrated the bread and wine they literally turned into living flesh and blood. It was an incredible miracle! The Church calls this a Eucharistic miracle.

Normally during Mass, we are unable to see the physical change from bread and wine to the Body and Blood of Christ. We have faith that the change takes place. But at this particular moment in time God decided to show the world what happens during every Mass.

Today, you can travel to Lanciano, Italy, where the miracle took place and see the flesh and the blood from that miracle over a thousand years ago.

Every time you go to Mass, the change from bread and wine to the Body and Blood of Jesus occurs. Jesus is truly present in the Eucharist. This is an incredible gift! You are blessed to be able to receive Jesus in the Eucharist.

From the Bible: The Last Supper

On the night before he died Jesus gathered his disciples for one last meal together. It was the Jewish feast of Passover.

While they were together at the table Jesus spoke to them about how he was going to be betrayed and suffer.

Then while they were eating, Jesus took a loaf of bread, and after blessing it, he broke it and gave it to his disciples, saying, "Take this, all of you, and eat it; this is my Body." Then he took a cup, and after giving thanks, he gave it to them, saying, "Take this, all of you, and drink from it; this is the cup of my Blood, which will be poured out for many, for the forgiveness of sins."

When they had finished their meal, they went out to the Mount of Olives.

Adapted from Matthew 26:26–30

This is known as the Last Supper, the most famous meal in the history of the world. At the Last Supper Jesus did something incredible. He turned ordinary bread and wine into his Body and Blood. The Last Supper was the first Eucharist, and the disciples' First Communion.

There in that room two thousand years ago, Jesus gave himself to the disciples. And every time we receive the Eucharist he gives himself to us in the same way!

Jesus wants to be invited into your life. He wants to be your friend. He wants to encourage you, guide you, listen to you, and love you. Jesus wants to help you become the-best-version-of-yourself, grow in virtue, and live a holy life. You are blessed!

Jesus Is in You

After you receive Jesus in the Eucharist you will make your way back to your seat. At this moment, Jesus is in you. Amazing!

If Jesus came to visit you at your house, imagine how you would prepare for his arrival, imagine how excited you would be for him to get there, and imagine how you would sit by him and listen to everything he had to say.

Well, not only does Jesus come to visit us in the Mass, but he makes his home within us when we receive the Eucharist. So, when you get back to your seat after receiving Jesus in the Eucharist, this is a very special time of prayer.

Kneel or sit down, close your eyes, and talk to Jesus in your heart. This is a very special moment. Jesus is inside you. Thank him for all the ways he has blessed you. Count your blessings, one by one, with Jesus.

The Eucharist energizes and nourishes your soul. You receive many gifts each time you receive the Eucharist. This is a short list of some of those gifts:

Friendship with Jesus
Desire to do the will of God
Cleansing of venial sin
Hunger for virtue
Grace to avoid sin in the future
A heart that listens to the Holy Spirit
Desire to know and love God

Your First Communion is a very important moment in your life, but every time we receive Jesus in the Eucharist is an incredible gift that we should never take for granted.

The Concluding Rites

After we have had a few quiet minutes of prayer with Jesus, it is time for the final prayer and blessing.

> **Priest: May Almighty God bless you, the Father, the Son, and the Holy Spirit.**
> **Congregation: Amen!**
> **Priest or Deacon: Go forth, the Mass is ended.**
> **Congregation: Thanks be to God!**

In the final blessing we are being sent forth. Sent to do what? God's work in the world. At the end of Mass, God sends you out on a mission. He has fed you with his Word and the Eucharist. He has provided you with everything you need to bring his love to the world you live in.

You are blessed and God wants you to go out into the world and share your blessings with others.

Show What You Know

True or False

1. _____ One of the great blessings God wants to share with you is the Eucharist.

2. _____ The Eucharist is uniquely Catholic.

3. _____ The bread and wine don't become the Body and Blood of Jesus.

4. _____ Our souls are not nourished by the Eucharist.

5. _____ Jesus is truly present in the Eucharist.

Fill in the blank

1. There are _____ of blessings God wants to shower upon you.

2. The _____ is food for your soul.

3. You are so blessed to be _____.

4. Receiving Holy Communion is an incredible _____ that we should never take for granted.

5. You are on a great _____ with God and your destination is _____.

6. The consecration is the moment when the bread and wine become the _____ and _____ of Jesus.

7. To consecrate the bread and wine, the priest says the same words Jesus used during the _____ _____.

8. God fills you with _____ so that you can go into the world and share it with everyone who crosses your path.

9. God _____ you so much that he sent his son, Jesus, so that you could have eternal life!

10. You are _____ and God wants you to go out into the world and share your_____ with others.

Word Bank

CATHOLIC	HEAVEN
BODY	BLOOD
BLESSINGS	JOURNEY
LAST SUPPER	LOVES
THOUSANDS	EUCHARIST
PEACE	BLESSED
GIFT	

Journal with Jesus

Dear Jesus,

I know you will never leave me because . . .

_____

_____

_____

_____

_____

_____

_____

Closing Prayer

There is so much to be discovered about the Mass. You could spend a lifetime going to Mass every single day, and at the end of your life still be surprised by the beautiful meaning behind everything we do and say at Mass.

Our God is a God of surprises. We can never put limits on what he is capable of or how his love can transform something ordinary, like bread and wine, into something truly extraordinary, like the Body and Blood of Jesus.

**Lord, catch me off guard today.
Surprise me with some moment
of beauty or pain.
So that at least for the moment I may be
startled into seeing that you are here in all your splendor,
always and everywhere, barely hidden, beneath, beyond,
within this life I breathe.**

Amen.

Frederick Buechner

5

Your First Communion

_____

God, our loving Father,
thank you for all the ways you bless me.
Help me to be aware that every person,
place, and adventure I experience is an
opportunity to love you more.
Fill me with a desire to change and to grow,
and give me the grace to become
the-best-version-of-myself in
every moment of every day.

Amen.

This Is a Special Day

Have you ever been excited to give someone a gift? Maybe it was at Christmas or perhaps it was for someone's birthday. When you're really excited to give someone a gift, it's hard to keep that gift a secret. It's even harder to wait until the day of celebration to give the gift. It might feel like you're about to burst because you're so excited!

This is how God the Father feels when he thinks about giving you Jesus in the Eucharist. He knows how special this gift is, and he can hardly wait to share it with you.

Your First Communion is a very special day. You are blessed!

On the morning of your First Communion, before you get dressed, before you receive any gifts, before you even have breakfast, begin the day quietly with God in prayer. Let's practice together now:

Loving Father, thank you for blessing me in so many ways. Jesus, I am looking forward to receiving you in the Eucharist for the very first time. Holy Spirit, help me to pay attention and make the most of this fabulous day.

Amen.

This is a very special day. You will remember your First Communion for the rest of your life. You are blessed!

You're Growing Up

When you think about all the things you can do today that you could not do one, two, or three years ago, you realize that you are growing up quickly.

One of the most significant signs that you are growing up is your ability to take responsibility for your own actions.

You are able to follow directions. For example, when parents or teachers ask you to do something, you are able to understand what they are asking and do it.

You are able to control your impulses. For example, when your brother or sister does something to upset you, you are able to control your anger. And you are able to listen to and follow your conscience. For instance, if a friend asks you to do something that is wrong you will hear your conscience advising you not to do it—and you are able to say no to your friend.

The Church chooses this time in your life to share the Eucharist with you because you have reached the age of reason. When we reach the age of reason we are able to determine the difference between right and wrong and take responsibility for our actions.

You are ready to say yes to God. You are ready to say no to anything that does not help you become the-best-version-of-yourself. You are ready to walk with God, and you are ready to receive Jesus in the Eucharist.

Preparation Matters

When you were preparing for your First Reconciliation we talked about how important preparation is. We Catholics prepare for everything that is important.

Just as great athletes prepare every time they compete, Catholics prepare for the biggest moments in life. The great champions of our faith are the saints. They are all masters at preparation. The saints teach us how to prepare to receive Jesus in the Eucharist.

You are preparing for your First Communion, but it is important to prepare every time we receive Jesus in the Eucharist. We do this with prayer and fasting.

Prayer

One of the best ways to prepare to receive Jesus is to pray. Prayer is a conversation with God. We all need a few minutes each day in a quiet place to sit and talk to him.

We continue our conversation with God throughout the day. When we see something amazing, we can say: "Wow, God, did you see that?" When we are afraid to do something that we know we should do, we can say: "God, please give me the courage to do this." And when something wonderful happens, we can say: "God, thank you for all the ways you bless me!"

Let's pray together right now, asking God to help us in the final preparations for our First Communion.

> **Loving Father, thank you for all the wonderful ways you bless me every day. Please prepare my mind, heart, and soul to receive your son Jesus in the Eucharist. And help me to always remember that you want the very best for me. Amen.**

Fasting

Another way we prepare to receive Jesus in the Eucharist is by abstaining from food for one hour before Mass. What does abstaining mean? It means going without. That's right, we don't eat or drink anything except water for one hour before Mass.

Fasting has played an important role in helping people grow spiritually for thousands of years. Our Jewish ancestors fasted to say sorry to God for their sins, to prepare for important events, and they fasted so they could see God's will more clearly. And Jesus went into the desert and fasted for forty days to prepare for his mission.

When you are an adult, the Church will invite you to fast on certain days, like Ash Wednesday and Good Friday. Right now, the Church invites you to fast for one hour before Mass.

Fasting makes us more mindful of God's presence. It reminds us of how dependent we are on God and helps us to hear his voice more clearly. Fasting reminds us of our spiritual hunger. It helps us grow closer to God.

Receiving Jesus in the Eucharist is an awesome privilege. We prepare with prayer and fasting.

Prayer, fasting, and receiving Jesus in the Eucharist all help us to become more perfectly the person God created us to be, to grow in virtue, and to live holy lives.

The Eucharist Empowers Us to Do Great Things

The Eucharist empowers us to do great things for God. For two thousand years Christians have been doing wonderful things.

The first Christians changed the world by showing everyone how to live in loving community. By setting aside selfishness and loving each other they became great witnesses to God's love and fulfilled Jesus' vision: "Everyone will know you are my disciples if you love one another" (John 13:35).

The Eucharist empowered the saints to do great things for God too. It inspired and empowered St. Ignatius of Loyola to create schools and universities.

St. Teresa of Calcutta used to sit before the Eucharist for an hour each day just talking to Jesus. It gave her the strength and courage to care for the poorest of the poor.

Jesus in the Eucharist gave St. Francis of Assisi the strength to rebuild the Church and the wisdom to help men, women, and children grow spiritually.

St. Thérèse of Lisieux received power from the Eucharist to do little things every day with great love.

The Eucharist gave St. Thomas Aquinas the ability to write great books that helped people discover the genius of the Catholic faith.

God has been using the Eucharist to empower people to do great things for two thousand years. I am so excited to see what the Eucharist empowers you to do with your life.

From the Bible: The Visitation

When Mary was pregnant with Jesus, she went to visit her cousin Elizabeth, who was pregnant with John the Baptist. As soon as Mary arrived at Elizabeth's house, baby John heard the voice of Mary and leapt with joy.

Elizabeth felt John dancing in her womb and the Holy Spirit helped her to say these now famous words: "Blessed are you among women, and blessed is the fruit of your womb! And why is this granted to me, that the mother of my Lord should come to me? For behold, when the voice of your greeting came to my ears, the babe in my womb leaped for joy" (Luke 1:42–44).

Mary then stayed with Elizabeth for three months before returning home.

Jesus was in Mary's womb. That's why the baby John danced for joy. He was so excited to be in Jesus' presence.

When you go to church there is usually a little red light on next to the tabernacle. This light means that Jesus is in the tabernacle. Mary was the first tabernacle; Jesus was inside her.

After you receive the Eucharist, Jesus will be in you. This should bring you great joy.

With Jesus alive within us, we are each called to go out into the world as his ambassadors and disciples. You can do this by being kind and generous. You can do it by living a holy life. You can do it by encouraging people.

God is sending you on a mission to bring his love to the world.

Your First but Not Your Last

This is your first but not your last Communion. Every Sunday when you go to Mass you can receive Jesus in the Eucharist. And if you are fortunate enough to go during the week for any reason, you can receive the Eucharist more than once a week. In fact, there are some people who go to Mass every day.

I want to encourage you to receive the Eucharist as often as you can, because the Eucharist fills us with the wisdom and courage to become the-best-version-of-ourselves, to grow in virtue, and to live the fabulous holy lives God wants us to live.

Just as we need to feed the body to give it the nourishment and energy it needs, we need to feed the soul too. We feed the soul with prayer, reading the Bible, and of course with the Eucharist, the ultimate food for the soul.

The Eucharist is a great blessing. You are blessed.

For the rest of your life you will have an open invitation to God's great banquet. God is the most generous host who has ever lived. He will never stop inviting you to share in this great celebration and he will never run out of food to nourish your soul.

There may be times when you wander away from God. But God will never stop calling you. He will never stop searching for you. God will never stop encouraging you to become the-best-version-of-yourself, grow in virtue, and live a holy life.

You are blessed.

Show What You Know

True or False

1. _____ Your First Communion is a very special day.

2. _____ You are not ready to walk with God, and you are not ready to receive Jesus in the Eucharist.

3. _____ Prayer doesn't help us prepare to receive Jesus in the Eucharist.

4. _____ Fasting makes us mindful of God's presence.

5. _____ For the rest of your life you will have an open invitation to God's great banquet.

Fill in the blank

1. God the Father is so _____ when he thinks about giving you Jesus in the Eucharist.

2. The Church chooses this time in your life to share the _____ with you because you have reached the age of reason.

3. We _____ for everything that is important.

4. The great champions of our faith are the _____.

5. Prayer is a _____ with God.

6. Fasting helps us to grow _____ to God.

7. The Eucharist fills us with the _____ and _____ to become the-best-version-of-ourselves, to grow in virtue, and to live a holy lives.

8. The Eucharist empowers us to do _____ things for God.

9. After you receive the Eucharist, _____ will be in you.

10. God is sending you on a _____ to bring his love to the world.

Word Bank

GREAT	EUCHARIST	CONVERSATION	WISDOM	MISSION
JESUS	EXCITED	COURAGE	CLOSER	PREPARE	SAINTS

Journal with Jesus

Dear Jesus,

I hope receiving you in the Eucharist inspires me to . . .

_____

_____

_____

_____

_____

_____

_____

_____

Closing Prayer

Throughout the Gospels we hear about Jesus performing incredible miracles. He made the lame walk and the blind see, fed the hungry, and even raised Lazarus from the dead.

Jesus has the power to transform everyone he comes into contact with. Sometimes that transformation comes in a single moment, but most of the time that transformation happens slowly over our lifetime.

If you stay close to Jesus in the Eucharist, the power of God will do incredible things in your life too. The Eucharist will open the eyes of your soul and cure it of selfishness and blindness, so you can love generously.

Let's pray together now:

> **My Lord and my God,**
> **I firmly believe that you are present in the Eucharist.**
> **Take the blindness from my eyes,**
> **So that I can see all people and things as you see them.**
> **Take the deafness from my ears,**
> **So that I can hear your truth and follow it.**
> **Take the hardness from my heart,**
> **So that I can live and love generously.**
> **Give me the grace to receive**
> **the Eucharist with humility,**
> **So that you can transform me a little more each day**
> **into the person you created me to be.**
>
> **Amen.**

6

God's Family

God, our loving Father,
thank you for all the ways you bless me.
Help me to be aware that every person,
place, and adventure I experience is an
opportunity to love you more.
Fill me with a desire to change and to grow,
and give me the grace to become
the-best-version-of-myself in
every moment of every day.

Amen.

Made for Mission

Now that you have discovered the healing power of God's forgiveness and the life-changing power of the Eucharist, it's a good time to think about why God has blessed you in so many ways.

God has blessed you because he loves you. He has blessed you because he wants you to live a fabulous life here on earth and to live in heaven with him forever. And God has blessed you because he made you for mission.

God gives every single person a mission. It may take some time to work out exactly what mission God is calling you to, but you have already learned about the most important part of your mission: to bring God's love to everyone you meet.

You were made for mission. God didn't make you just to have fun. He didn't create you to waste your time on things that are superficial. God made you for mission.

Your Parish Family

Did you know you belong to the most famous family in the world? That's right. You are blessed to be a member of the Catholic Church, and the Catholic Church is the most famous family in the world.

In almost every place around the world you can find a Catholic Church. You experience the Church through your local parish. Your parish is made up of men, women, and children just like you, who are all trying to become the-best-version-of-themselves and live holy lives.

When you were a baby your family took care of you. They fed you, cleaned you, and made sure you had what you needed to grow healthy and strong. Your parish feeds your soul. Your parish makes sure you have what you need to grow spiritually. Your parish helped you prepare for your First Reconciliation and your First Communion, so that you can be ready for the great mission God dreamed for you.

Throughout your life, there are going to be moments of great joy and moments of disappointment, failure, and sadness. All these experiences are part of life. We all experience them. But our spiritual family, our parish, is there for us through it all to comfort and care for us.

You are blessed! The Catholic Church is the greatest force for good in the world. Every day your Catholic family feeds millions of people all around the world. Through your generosity and mine together, we are able to give housing to the homeless and clothing for those who have none and take care of sick people in every country around the world.

Do you know why the Catholic Church does all this?

We do it because we are all God's children. We are one big family. We have been given the mission to bring God's love to every person on earth. And families take care of one another. The Catholic Church is the biggest family in the world, and you are a part of it.

You are blessed to be Catholic.

Your parish is blessed to have you. I am excited to see the ways you use your talents to serve your parish. You see, your parish needs you. Without you, there would be a big hole in your parish. Your parish is helping you become the-best-version-of-yourself, but it also needs you to help it become the-best-version-of-itself.

That's right, God needs every parish in the world to be the-best-version-of-itself so that together they can powerfully serve every single person on earth. That's a big mission, isn't it?

Before Jesus ascended into heaven he said to his disciples, "Go out into the world and share my love and my message with every person in every country" (Matthew 28:19). He gives this same mission to you and me today. He wants us to share his love and his message with the world.

Go Make a Difference

Once upon a time, there was a boy who lived by the ocean. Every afternoon he would walk along the beach. One day he noticed that as the tide had gone out it had left hundreds of starfish stranded on the sand. He realized the starfish would die if they were left there, so he started to pick them up one by one and throw them back into the water.

As the boy got to the other end of the beach, an old man came walking from the other direction. He saw what the boy was doing and said, "What are you doing, boy? You'll never make a difference. Why don't you just enjoy your walk?"

The boy ignored the old man and continued to pick the starfish up, one at a time, and throw them back into the water. But as the old man got closer, he came up to the boy and said, "You're wasting your time, boy. There are hundreds of them, maybe thousands. And there will be more tomorrow. You'll never make a difference."

The boy smiled, reached down in the sand, picked up one more starfish from the sand, and threw it as far as he could out into the ocean. Then he turned to the old man and said, "I made a difference for that one!"

You may be a great football player or a fabulous singer, but your greatest talent is your ability to make a difference in other people's lives. You will be amazed how you can bring joy to others by using this talent.

As disciples of Jesus we should always be looking for ways to make a difference in other people's lives. This is one of the ways we live out the mission that God has given us to bring his love to the world.

Just like the old man in the story, there will be people who try to discourage you. But the Holy Spirit is constantly encouraging you, saying, "You can do it!" "You're amazing!" "You can make a difference!" "You've got what it takes!"

There will be times when you cannot do everything. For example, there are millions of hungry people in the world. You cannot feed them all, but you might be able to help feed one. Don't let what you can't do interfere with what you can do. Do your little bit. If everyone does their own little bit, we will change the world.

Jesus has given himself to you in the Eucharist. Now Jesus is sending you out into the world on a mission. There is a song we sing at church sometimes that perfectly summarizes this mission. It is called "Go Make a Difference." Here are some of the lyrics:

Go make a difference; we can make a difference
Go make a difference in the world
Go make a difference; you can make a difference
Go make a difference in the world.

The Power of Prayer

Another powerful way for us to make a difference is by praying for other people. Prayer is powerful. Prayer makes a difference.

Perhaps you hear about a tornado on the other side of the world that has destroyed homes and fields, and now the people are hungry and homeless. You cannot go there and help them, and you may have no money to send them. But you can always pray for them.

Each day our prayer should be a great adventure that takes us all around the world. The adventure of prayer may begin in your own home, praying for your family; then perhaps you pray for your grandparents in California, or New York, or Florida; then you pray for a friend who moved to a new city; then you pray for the pope, in Rome; then you pray for the hungry children in Africa, and the people who were hurt in an earthquake in China. Prayer is a chance to travel all around the world.

And our prayer is not even limited to this world. We also pray for the souls in purgatory. Imagine being in purgatory and having nobody to pray for you. That would be quite sad, so we should each take a moment every day to pray for the souls in purgatory.

Prayer is a powerful way to make a difference. We can and should pray for ourselves, thanking God for all the ways he has blessed us and asking him to give us what we need to fulfill the mission he has given us here on earth. And we can and should pray for other people every day of our lives.

You are blessed, and you can bless others by praying for them.

From the Bible: I Will Be With You Always

On Good Friday when Jesus was hanging on the cross, the disciples were sad and confused. They had placed all their hope in Jesus and now he was dead.

The disciples loved Jesus. He had been their teacher and their friend. They'd had great expectations that he would be the one sent from God to save them, just like they had read about in the Scriptures. But now he was gone and they felt deserted and alone.

Imagine how long Friday night was for them. They probably couldn't sleep, thinking about everything that had happened, wondering what would happen next. They were probably afraid that the people who had killed Jesus might try to kill them too.

I wonder what they did on Saturday. I wonder what they thought and what they said to each other. That Friday and Saturday were the worst days of their lives.

But on Sunday morning everything changed. Jesus rose from the dead. He had told them he would, but maybe they didn't understand, or maybe they forgot, or maybe they didn't believe!

When Jesus rose from the dead and appeared to the disciples, you can imagine how amazed and excited they were.

Over the next forty days Jesus appeared to many people, to encourage them in their mission and remind them of his great love.

When it was time for Jesus to ascend into heaven, he had a very important message for us all. He said to the disciples, "I am going now to be with my Father in heaven, but wherever you are in this world, I will always be with you at your side."

Adapted from Matthew 28:20

Jesus has been keeping this promise for two thousand years. He is waiting for you to get out of bed when you wake up in the morning. He rides with you to school. He is there in class and on the playground. He cheers for you at soccer and baseball. And he tucks you into bed at night and kisses you on your forehead.

Jesus loves you and he wants to be with you.

He is also with us always in the Eucharist. Every time you visit a church and see that little red light on beside the tabernacle, Jesus is there with you in a very special way.

Life is difficult, and we often have to make big decisions. When I have to make a decision, I like to stop by church and sit with Jesus in the tabernacle and talk to him. I talk to him about the decision I need to make, and I ask him for his advice. Then I sit quietly and let him speak to my heart.

Jesus wants you to remember that he is always there for you. Whatever challenges come your way in life, you are never alone; Jesus is at your side. He is your friend and your teacher.

You are blessed!

Trusting God

Our God is a God of purpose. He does things on purpose and he made you for a purpose.

As you journey through life, look for the purpose in things. Eating is fun and pleasurable, but the purpose of food is to fuel the body. Going to school and seeing your friends is great, but the purpose of school is to learn new things. Winning at soccer is exciting, but the purpose of sports is to help us grow strong and stay healthy.

By realizing that God has a purpose for everything, we learn to trust him and the beautiful plans he has for our lives. Keep your eye on the purpose of things. If you are ever confused, ask God, "What is the purpose of . . . ?"

The Bible tells us that there is a time for everything. There is a time to laugh and a time to cry, a time to sow and a time to reap, a time to be born and a time to die, a time to rejoice and a time to mourn, a time to speak and a time to listen. And it is always a good time to trust in God and the beautiful plans he has for your life (Ecclesiastes 3:1).

This is a time for you to celebrate. Your First Communion is one of the great moments in your life. The Eucharist will help you become the-best-version-of-yourself, grow in virtue, and live a holy life.

There may be times in your life when you feel like God is far away, but he is not. There may be times in your life when you feel that God has forgotten you, but he will never forget you. He is with you always, at your side.

Life is a wonderful journey. Anytime you feel lost or confused, turn to Jesus and ask him to guide you and comfort you. The Eucharist reminds us that God is with us and that he wants to take care of us.

There is a time for everything and a purpose for everything. Place your trust in God. Throughout the day, a very simple prayer to repeat is: Jesus, I trust in you.

Pray it over and over and over again. "Jesus, I trust in you. Jesus, I trust in you. Jesus, I trust in you."

It has been a pleasure joining you for this part of your journey. Everyone at Dynamic Catholic is praying for you every day. We hope the lessons you have learned preparing for your First Reconciliation and your First Communion will live with you forever.

You are blessed. Blessed to be Catholic, blessed to be alive, and blessed to be loved. Try to remind yourself of that each day. Each morning when you wake up, and each night when you go to bed, whisper quietly to yourself, "I am blessed."

Show What You Know

True or False

1. _____ God has blessed you because he loves you.

2. _____ Your parish doesn't need you to spread God's love.

3. _____ Prayer is a powerful way to make a difference.

4. _____ Jesus asks us to face life's journey alone.

5. _____ You are blessed.

Fill in the blank

1. God made you for _____.

2. The Catholic Church is the greatest force for _____ in the world.

3. Our mission is to bring God's _____ to every person on earth.

4. Your _____ is your spiritual family.

5. Your greatest talent is your ability to make a _____ in other people's lives.

6. Every day our _____ should be a great adventure that takes us all around the world.

7. Our God is a God of _____.

8. The _____ _____ will help you become the-best-version-of-yourself, grow in virtue, and live a holy life.

9. Anytime you feel lost or confused, turn to _____ and ask him to guide you and comfort you.

10. You are Catholic, you are alive, you are loved, and you are _____!

Word Bank

| PRAYER | PARISH | EUCHARIST | MISSION | BLESSED |
| GOOD | JESUS | LOVE | PURPOSE | DIFFERENCE |

Journal with Jesus

Dear Jesus,

I want to spread your love because . . .

_____

_____

_____

_____

_____

_____

_____

Closing Prayer

Explorers carry compasses so they don't get lost. A compass is a tool with a little arrow on it that always points North. Even if you have no idea where you are, your compass will help you find your way home.

Life is a great journey. You are an explorer and Jesus is your compass. There will be times when you don't know what to do next. Turn to Jesus during those times; he wants to help you live an amazing life.

And remember, you are not the first one to make this great journey, and you are not alone. Just as you are praying for other people, there are some great people praying for you. The angels and saints are in heaven cheering for you and praying for you. Every time you make a decision, they are praying you make a great choice and, with God's help, become the-best-version-of-yourself.

So, let's pray with the angels and saints to finish our time together:

Loving Father, thank you for all the ways you bless me.
Inspire me to share your love
with everyone who crosses my path.
Never let me forget that you are always with me.

Holy Mary, Mother of God, pray for us.
Saint Michael, the Archangel, pray for us.
Saint John the Baptist, pray for us.
Saint Joseph, pray for us.
Saint Peter, pray for us.
Saint Paul, pray for us.
Saint Matthew, pray for us.
Saint Mary Magdalene, pray for us.
Saint Anthony, pray for us.
Saint Francis, pray for us.
Saint Clare, pray for us.
Saint Catherine, pray for us.
All holy men and women of God, pray for us.

Amen.

My Little Catechism

Your fabulous journey with God is just beginning. Along the way you will have many questions. Questions are good. God places questions in your heart and mind for many different reasons. Follow your questions, wherever they might lead you.

Some of your questions will be easy to find answers to. To help us answer many of our questions, our spiritual leaders have given us the Catechism of the Catholic Church. The answers we find there have been revealed by God and by nature over the centuries.

In the pages that follow we will share with you some questions you may have about God and life. The answers are easy to read but often hard to live. But the answers will help you become the-best-version-of-yourself, grow in virtue, and live a holy life.

There will be other times in your life when you have questions that cannot be answered by words on a page, for example what Vocation you are called to or what career you should pursue. At these times you will seek deeply personal answers to deeply personal questions.

These questions require a lot more patience. Seek the advice of wise people who love the Lord. Read what wise men and women before you have had to say on such topics. But, most of all, pray and ask God to show you his way.

As you make this journey you will encounter others who have questions. Help them as best you can to find the answers. People deserve answers to their questions.

And never, ever, forget . . . you are blessed!

1. **Q: Who made you?**

   A: God made you.

   > In the Bible: Genesis 1:1, 26–27; Genesis 2:7, 21–22
   > In the Catechism: CCC 355

2. **Q: Does God love you?**

   A: Yes. God loves you more than anyone in the world,
   and more than you could ever imagine.

   > In the Bible: John 3:16
   > In the Catechism: CCC 457, 458

3. **Q: Why did God make you?**

   A: God made you to know him, love him, to carry out the mission he entrusts to
   you in this world, and to be happy with Him forever in Heaven.

   > In the Bible: Deuteronomy 10:12–15; John 17:3
   > In the Catechism: CCC 1, 358

4. **Q: What is God?**

   A: God is an infinite and perfect spirit.

   > In the Bible: Exodus 3:6; Isaiah 44:6; 1 John 4:8, 16
   > In the Catechism: CCC 198–200, 212, 221

5. **Q: Did God have a beginning?**

   A: No. God has no beginning. He always was and he always will be.

   > In the Bible: Psalm 90:2; Revelation 1:8
   > In the Catechism: CCC 202

6. **Q: Where is God?**

   A: Everywhere

   > In the Bible: Psalm 139
   > In the Catechism: CCC 1

7. **Q: Does God see us?**

   A: God sees us and watches over us.

   > In the Bible: Wisdom 11:24–26; Jeremiah 1:5
   > In the Catechism: CCC 37, 301, 302

8. **Q: Does God know everything?**

   A: Yes. God knows all things, even our most secret thoughts, words, and actions.

   In the Bible: Job 21:22; Psalm 33:13–15; Psalm 147:4–5
   In the Catechism: CCC 208

9. **Q: Is God all loving, just, holy, and merciful?**

   A: Yes, God is loving, all just, all holy, and all merciful—and he invites us to be loving, just, holy, and merciful too.

   In the Bible: John 13:34; 1 John 4:8; Ephesians 2:4
   In the Catechism: CCC 214, 211, 208

10. **Q: Is there only one God?**

    A: Yes, there is only one God.

    In the Bible: Isaiah 44:6; John 8:58
    In the Catechism: CCC 253

11. **Q: Why is there only one God?**

    A: There can only be one God, because God, being supreme and infinite, cannot have an equal.

    In the Bible: Mark 12:29–30
    In the Catechism: CCC 202

12. **Q: How many Persons are there in God?**

    A: In God there are three Divine Persons, unique and distinct and yet equal in all things—the Father, the Son, and the Holy Spirit.

    In the Bible: 1 Corinthians 12:4–6; 2 Corinthians 13:13; Ephesians 4:4–6
    In the Catechism: CCC 252, 254, 255

13. **Q: Is the Father God?**

    A: Yes.

    In the Bible: Exodus 3:6; Exodus 4:22
    In the Catechism: CCC 253, 262

14. **Q: Is the Son God?**

    A: Yes.

    In the Bible: John 8:58; John 10:30
    In the Catechism: CCC 253, 262

15. **Q: Is the Holy Spirit God?**

A: Yes.

In the Bible: John 14:26; John 15:26
In the Catechism: CCC 253, 263

16. **Q: What is the Holy Trinity?**

A: The Holy Trinity is one God in three divine persons—Father, Son, and Holy Spirit.

In the Bible: Matthew 28:19
In the Catechism CCC 249, 251

17. **Q. What is free will?**

A: Free will is an incredible gift from God that allows us to make our own decisions. This incredible gift comes with incredible responsibility.

In the Bible: Sirach 15:14—15
In the Catechism: CCC 1731

18. **Q. What is sin?**

A: Sin is any willful thought, word, deed, or omission contrary to the law of God.

In the Bible: Genesis 3:5; Exodus 20:1—17
In the Catechism: CCC 1850

19. **Q: How many kinds of sin are there?**

A: There are two actual kinds of sin—venial and mortal.

In the Bible: 1 John 5:16—17
In the Catechism: CCC 1855

20. **Q: What is a venial sin?**

A: Venial is a slight offense against God.

In the Bible: Matthew 5:19; Matthew 12:32; 1 John 5:16—18
In the Catechism: CCC 1855, 1863

21. **Q: What is a mortal sin?**

A: Mortal sin is a grievous offense against God and his law.

In the Bible: Matthew 12:32; 1 John 5:16—18
In the Catechism: CCC 1855, 1857

22. **Q: Does God abandon us when we sin?**

A: Never. God is always calling to us, pleading with us, to return to him and his ways.

In the Bible: Psalm 103: 9–10, 13; Jeremiah 3:22; Matthew 28:20; Luke 15:11-32
In the Catechism: CCC 27, 55, 982

23. **Q: Which Person of the Holy Trinity became man?**

A: The Second Person, God the Son, became man without giving up his divine nature.

In the Bible: 1 John 4:2
In the Catechism: CCC 423,464

24. **Q: What name was given to the Second Person of the Holy Trinity when he became man?**

A: Jesus.

In the Bible: Luke 1:31; Matthew 1:21
In the Catechism: CCC 430

25. **Q: When the Son became man, did he have a human mother?**

A: Yes.

In the Bible: Luke 1:26–27
In the Catechism: CCC 488, 490, 495

26. **Q: Who was Jesus' mother?**

A: The Blessed Virgin Mary.

In the Bible: Luke 1:30, 31; Matthew 1:21–23
In the Catechism: CCC 488, 495

27. **Q: Why do we honor Mary?**

A: Because she is the mother of Jesus and our mother too.

In the Bible: Luke 1:48; John 19:27
In the Catechism: CCC 971

28. **Q: Who was Jesus' real father?**

A: God the Father.

In the Bible: Luke 1:35; John 17:1
In the Catechism CCC 422, 426, 442

29. **Q: Who was Jesus' foster father?**

A: Joseph.

In the Bible: Matthew 1:19, 20; Matthew 2:13, 19—21
In the Catechism: CCC 437, 488, 1655

30. **Q: Is Jesus God, or is he man, or is he both God and man?**

A: Jesus is both God and man; as the Second Person of the Holy Trinity, he is God; and since he took on a human nature from his mother Mary, he is man.

In the Bible: Philippians 2: 6-7; John 1:14, 16; John 13:3; 1 John 4:2
In the Catechism: CCC 464, 469

31. **Q: Was Jesus also a man?**

A: Yes, Jesus was fully God and fully human.

In the Bible: Luke 24:39; 1 John 4:2—3
In the Catechism: CCC 464, 469, 470

32. **Q: On what day was Jesus born?**

A: Jesus was born on Christmas day in a stable in Bethlehem.

In the Bible: Luke 2:1—20; Matthew 1:18—25
In the Catechism: CCC 437, 563

33. **Q: What is the Incarnation?**

A: The Incarnation is the belief that Jesus became man.

In the Bible: John 1:14; 1 John 4:2
In the Catechism: CCC 461, 463

34. **Q: Did Jesus love life?**

A: Yes.

In the Bible: John 10:10; John 2:1—12
In the Catechism: CCC 221, 257, 989

35. **Q: If Jesus loved life why did he willingly die on the cross?**

A: He died on the cross because he loved you and me even more than life.

In the Bible: Romans 5:8; John 15:13; Ephesians 5:2
In the Catechism: CCC 1825, 604

36. **Q: Why did Jesus suffer and die?**

    A: So that we could be forgiven our sins, and live with him in heaven forever after this life.

    > In the Bible: John 3:16; 2 Corinthians 5:14–16
    > In the Catechism: CCC 604, 618, 620

37. **Q: What do we call the mystery of God becoming man?**

    A: The mystery of the Incarnation.

    > In the Bible: John 1:14; 1 John 4:2
    > In the Catechism: CCC 461, 463

38. **Q: On what day did Jesus die on the cross?**

    A: Good Friday, the day after the Last Supper.

    > In the Bible: John 19:16–40; Matthew 27:33–50
    > In the Catechism CCC 641

39. **Q: On what day did Jesus rise from the dead?**

    A: On Easter Sunday, three days after Good Friday.

    > In the Bible: Matthew 28:1–6; Mark 16:1–8
    > In the Catechism: CCC 1169, 1170

40. **Q: What gifts do we receive as a result of being saved by Jesus?**

    A: By dying on the cross Jesus restored our relationship with God and opened a floodgate of grace.

    > In the Bible: Luke 23:44–46; Romans 3:21–26; 2 Corinthians 5:17–21
    > In the Catechism: CCC 1026, 1047

41. **Q: What is grace?**

    A: Grace is the help God gives us to respond generously to his call, to do what is good and right, grow in virtue, and live holy lives.

    > In the Bible: John 1:12–18; 2 Corinthians 12:9
    > In the Catechism: CCC 1996

42. **Q: What is Faith?**

    A: Faith is a gift from God. It is a supernatural virtue that allows us to firmly believe all the truth that God has revealed to us.

    > In the Bible: Hebrews 11:1
    > In the Catechism: CCC 1814

43. **Q: What is Hope?**

A: Hope is a gift from God. It is a supernatural virtue that allows us to firmly trust that God will keep all his promises and lead us to heaven.

In the Bible: Romans 8:24–25; 1 Timothy 4:10; 1 Timothy 1:1; Hebrews 6:18–20
In the Catechism: CCC 1817, 1820–1821

44. **Q: What is Charity?**

A: Charity is a gift from God. It is a supernatural virtue that allows us to love God above everything else, and our neighbor as ourselves.

In the Bible: John 13:34; 1 Corinthians 13:4–13
In the Catechism: CCC 1822, 1823, 1825

45. **Q: Will God give you the gifts of Faith, Hope, and Charity?**

A: Yes, God gives the gifts of Faith, Hope, and Charity, freely to all those who ask for them sincerely and consistently.

In the Bible: 1 Corinthians 13:13
In the Catechism: 1813

46. **Q: How long will God love me for?**

A: God will love you forever.

In the Bible: John 13:1; Romans 8:35–39
In the Catechism: CCC 219

47. **Q: When did Jesus ascend into heaven?**

A: On Ascension Thursday, forty days after Easter.

In the Bible: Acts 1:9; Mark 16:19
In the Catechism: CCC 659

48. **Q: When did the Holy Spirit descend upon the Apostles?**

A: On Pentecost Sunday, fifty days after Easter.

In the Bible: John 20:21–22; Matthew 28:19
In the Catechism: CCC 731, 1302

49. **Q: What is meant by the Redemption?**

A: Redemption means that Jesus' Incarnation, life, death, and Resurrection paid the price for our sins, opened the gates of heaven, and freed us from slavery to sin and death.

In the Bible: Ephesians 1:7; Romans 4:25
In the Catechism CCC 517, 606, 613

50. **Q: What did Jesus establish to continue his mission of Redemption?**

A: He established the Catholic Church.

In the Bible: Matthew 16:18
In the Catechism: CCC 773, 778, 817, 822

51. **Q: Why do we believe that the Catholic Church is the one true Church?**

A: Because it is the only Church established by Jesus.

In the Bible: Matthew 16:18
In the Catechism: CCC 750

52. **Q: Does it matter to which Church or religion you belong?**

A: Yes, in order to be faithful to Jesus, it is necessary to remain in the Church he established.

In the Bible: Mark 16:16; John 3:5
In the Catechism: CCC 846

53. **Q: What are the Four Marks of the Church?**

A: One, Holy, Catholic, and Apostolic.

In the Bible: Ephesians 2:20, 4:3, 5:26; Matthew 28:19; Revelation 21:14;
In the Catechism: CCC 813, 823, 830, 857

54. **Q: How does the Church preserve the teachings of Jesus?**

A: Through Sacred Scripture and Sacred Tradition.

In the Bible: 2 Timothy 2:2; 2 Thessalonians 2:15
In the Catechism: CCC 78, 81, 82

55. **Q: How does the Church's calendar differ from the secular calendar?**

A: The first day of the Church's year is the first Sunday of Advent, not January 1st. The Church's calendar revolves around the life, death, and Resurrection of Jesus. Throughout the course of the Church's year the whole mystery of Jesus Christ is unfolded.

In the Bible: Luke 2:1–20; 1 Corinthians 15:3–4
In the Catechism: CCC 1163; 1171, 1194

Going Deeper

Over the course of the year, through the readings at Mass, the feast days and holy days, we experience the story of Jesus. The Church's calendar does this to remind us that Jesus' story is not just about what happened over two thousand years ago. It is about our friendship with him today. The mystery of his life, teachings, and saving grace are unfolding in your life and the life of the Church today.

56. Q: Did Jesus give special authority to one of the Apostles?

A: Yes, to Peter when Jesus said to him, "I will give you the keys of the kingdom of heaven, and whatever you bind on earth shall be bound in heaven, and whatever you loose on earth shall be loosed in heaven."

In the Bible: Mark 3:16, 9:2; Luke 24:34
In the Catechism: CCC 552, 881

57. Q: Who speaks with the authority that Jesus gave to St. Peter?

A: The pope who is St. Peter's successor, the Bishop of Rome, and the Vicar of Christ on earth.

In the Bible: Matthew 16:18; John 21:15–17
In the Catechism: CCC 891

58. Q: What is the name of the present pope?

A: Pope Francis.

In the Bible: Matthew 16:18; John 21:15–17
In the Catechism: CCC 936

59. Q: What is the sacred liturgy?

A: The Church's public worship of God.

In the Bible: John 4:23–24
In the Catechism: CCC 1069, 1070

60. Q: What attitude should we have when we participate in the sacred liturgy?

A: We should have the attitude of reverence in our hearts and respect in our actions and appearance.

In the Bible: Hebrews 12:28
In the Catechism: CCC 2097

61. Q: What is a Sacrament?

A: A Sacrament is an outward sign, instituted by Christ and entrusted to the Church to give grace. Grace bears fruit in those who receive them with the required dispositions.

In the Bible: 2 Peter 1:4
In the Catechism: CCC 1131

Going Deeper

God gives you grace to help you do what is good and right. When you are open
to God, he also gives you the grace to be kind, generous, courageous, and
compassionate toward others. Grace bears good fruit in our lives. One of the
most powerful ways God shares his grace with us is through the Sacraments.
This grace helps us to become the-very-best-version-of-ourselves, grow in
virtue, and live holy lives.

62. **Q: How does Jesus share his life with us?**

A: During his earthly life, Jesus shared his life with others through his words and
actions; now he shares the very same life with us through the Sacraments.

In the Bible: John 3:16; John 6:5–7
In the Catechism: CCC 521; 1131, 1115–1116

Going Deeper

God loves to share his life and love with us. We can experience his life through
daily prayer, Scripture, and through serving one another. The most powerful
way that God shares his life with us is through the Sacraments. Sunday Mass
and regular Reconciliation are two Sacraments that guide us and encourage us
on our journey to become the-best-version-of-ourselves, grow in virtue, and
live holy lives.

63. **Q: How many Sacraments are there?**

A: Seven.

In the Bible: John 20:22–23; Luke 22:14–20; John 7:37–39; James 5:14–16; Hebrews 5:1–6; Matthew 19:6
In the Catechism: CCC 1113

64. **Q: What are the Seven Sacraments; and which ones have you received?**

A: Baptism, Penance, Holy Eucharist, Confirmation, Holy Orders, Matrimony,
Anointing of the Sick. You have received Baptism, Penance, and Holy Eucharist.

In the Bible: John 20:22–23; Luke 22:14–20; John 7:37–39; James 5:14–16; Hebrews 5:1–6; Matthew 19:6;
In the Catechism: CCC 1113

65. **Q: What are the Sacraments you can only receive once?**

A: Baptism, Confirmation, and Holy Orders.

In the Bible: Ephesians 4:30
In the Catechism: CCC 1272

66. Q: **How is Christian initiation accomplished?**

A: Christian initiation is accomplished with three Sacraments: Baptism which is the beginning of new life; Confirmation which strengthens our new life in Christ; and the Eucharist which nourishes the disciple with Jesus' Body and Blood so that we can be transformed in Christ.

In the Bible: John 3:5; Acts 8:14–17; John 6:51–58
In the Catechism: CCC 1212; 1275

Going Deeper

Life is a journey with God. Baptism, Confirmation and First Communion are all great moments in your journey. They are Sacraments that work together to help you live your best life. In Baptism you receive new life in Jesus, in Confirmation God reminds us that he has a special mission for each and every single one of us, and Holy Communion gives us the strength and the wisdom to live that mission by serving God and others.

67. Q: **When you were born, did you have Sanctifying Grace (a share in God's life)?**

A: No.

In the Bible: Colossians 1:12–14
In the Catechism: CCC 403, 1250

68. Q: **Why are we not born with Sanctifying Grace?**

A: Because we are born with original sin which is the loss of Sanctifying Grace.

In the Bible: Genesis 3:23
In the Catechism: CCC 403, 1250

69. Q: **Was any human person conceived without original sin?**

A: Yes, Mary at her Immaculate Conception.

In the Bible: Luke 1:28
In the Catechism: CCC 491, 492

70. Q: **What was the original sin?**

A: Adam and Eve were tempted by the devil; and they chose to distrust God's goodness and to disobey his law.

In the Bible: Genesis 3:1–11; Romans 5:19
In the Catechism: CCC 397

71. **Q: Is there really a devil?**

A: Yes.

> In the Bible: 1 John 5:19; 1 Peter 5:8
> In the Catechism: CCC 391

72. **Q: Is it easier to be bad or to be good?**

A: It is easier to be bad, because original sin has left us with an inclination to sin called concupiscence.

> In the Bible: Romans 7:15–18
> In the Catechism: CCC 409, 1264, 2516

73. **Q: When did you receive Sanctifying Grace for the first time?**

A: At Baptism.

> In the Bible: 2 Corinthians 5:17
> In the Catechism: CCC 1265

74. **Q: What is Baptism?**

A: Baptism is the Sacrament of rebirth in Jesus that is necessary for salvation.

> In the Bible: 2 Corinthians 5:17; 2 Peter 1:4; Galatians 4:5–7;
> In the Catechism: CCC 1266, 1277, 1279

Going Deeper

Baptism is a great blessing. Through your Baptism you became a member of the Catholic Church. This is another wonderful reason why being Catholic is a great blessing. Through your Baptism, you received new life in Jesus. You were made for mission. God had that mission in mind when you were baptized, and every day since he has been preparing you for your mission. We discover that mission through prayer, the Sacraments, and service to others. God doesn't reveal our mission all at once, he reveals it step-by-step.

75. **Q: What are the fruits of Baptism?**

A: Baptism makes us Christians, cleanses us of original sin and personal sin, and reminds us that we are children of God and members of the Body of Christ— the Church.

> In the Bible: Galatians 4:5–7
> In the Catechism: CCC 1279

Going Deeper

In Baptism God gives us many gifts. We become Christian, our sins are forgiven, we are given new life in Jesus, and God marks us for a great mission. God is able to do this through the power of the Holy Spirit. In Baptism our souls are flooded with the gift of the Holy Spirit, which helps us in our journey to grow closer to God. Each and every Sacrament we receive is full of gifts, big and small. Every blessing reminds us that we are all sons and daughters of a loving Father.

76. **Q: What did Baptism do for you?**

A: It gave me a share in God's life for the first time, made me a child of God, and took away original sin.

In the Bible: 2 Corinthians 5:17; 2 Peter 1:4; Galatians 4:5–7
In the Catechism: CCC 1266, 1279

77. **Q: How old does someone need to be to receive Baptism?**

A: A person can be baptized at any age. Since the earliest times of Christianity, Baptism has been administered to infant children because Baptism is a grace and a gift that is freely given by God and does not presuppose any human merit.

In the Bible: Acts 2:37–39
In the Catechism: CCC 1282

Going Deeper

God's love is a free gift. There is nothing you could do to earn or lose God's love. You may be tempted to think that God's love is something to be earned. This is simply not true. God loved you into life, and God loved you into the Church. You did nothing to be born, and if you were baptized as an infant you did nothing to be baptized. You didn't do anything to deserve life or Baptism. God freely gives you life and faith.

78. **Q: Who administers the Sacrament of Baptism?**

A: Anyone can administer the Sacrament of Baptism in an emergency by pouring water over that person's head and saying, "I baptize you in the name of the Father, and of the Son, and of the Holy Spirit." Baptism, however, is usually administered by a priest or deacon.

In the Bible: Matthew 28:19
In the Catechism: CCC 1284

Going Deeper

Not everyone is baptized as an infant. Some people don't learn about Jesus until they are adults. But God wants everyone to receive the blessing of Baptism. He wants everyone to be a part of his family—the Catholic Church. He wants everyone to be free from original sin. He wants everyone to have new life in his Son Jesus. He wants everyone to spend eternity with him in heaven.

79. **Q: How long do you remain a child of God?**
   A: Forever.

   In the Bible: 1 Peter 1:3–4
   In the Catechism: CCC 1272, 1274

80. **Q: Can you lose a share in God's life after Baptism?**
   A: Yes.

   In the Bible: Mark 3:29
   In the Catechism: CCC 1861

81. **Q: Can we lose the new life of grace that God has freely given us?**
   A: Yes. The new life of grace can be lost by sin.

   In the Bible:1 Corinthians 6:9; 2 Corinthians 5:19–21; 1 John 1:9
   In the Catechism: CCC 1420

Going Deeper

At Baptism we are filled with a very special grace. This grace blesses us with new life and brings us into friendship with God. That new life can be hurt or lost when we sin. When that happens, don't worry because God has given us the blessing of Reconciliation! As long as we are truly sorry for our sins and go to Reconciliation, we can once again experience the fullness of life with God. Reconciliation is a great blessing!

82. **Q: How can you lose Sanctifying Grace (a share in God's life)?**
   A: By committing mortal sin.

   In the Bible: Galatians 5:19–21; Romans 1:28–32
   In the Catechism: CCC 1861

83. **Q: Which is the worse sin: venial or mortal?**
   A: Mortal (deadly) sin.

In the Bible: 1 John 5:16
In the Catechism: CCC 1855, 1874, 1875

84. Q: **What three things are necessary to commit a mortal sin?**
     A: 1. You must disobey God in a serious matter.
        2. You must know that it is wrong.
        3. You must freely choose to do it anyway.

In the Bible: Mark 10:19; Luke 16:19—31; James 2:10-11
In the Catechism: CCC 1857

85. Q: **What happens to you if you die in a state of mortal sin?**
     A: You go to hell.

In the Bible: 1 John 3:14—15; Matthew 25:41—46;
In the Catechism: CCC 1035, 1472, 1861, 1874

86. Q: **Is there really a hell?**
     A: Yes; it is the place of eternal separation from God.

In the Bible: Isaiah 66:24; Mark 9:47, 48
In the Catechism: CCC 1035

87. Q: **What happens if you die with venial sin on your soul?**
     A: You go to purgatory where you are purified and made perfect.

In the Bible: 1 Corinthians 3:14—15; 2 Maccabees 12:45—46
In the Catechism: CCC 1030, 1031, 1472

88. Q: **What happens to the souls in purgatory after their purification?**
     A: They go to heaven.

In the Bible: 2 Maccabees 12:45
In the Catechism: CCC 1030

89. Q: **Is there really a heaven?**
     A: Yes; it is the place of eternal happiness with God.

In the Bible: 1 John 3:2; 1 Corinthians 13:12; Revelation 22:4—5
In the Catechism: CCC 1023, 1024

90. Q: **Can any sin, no matter how serious, be forgiven?**
     A: Yes, any sin, no matter how serious or how many times it is committed
        can be forgiven.

In the Bible: Matthew 18:21—22
In the Catechism: CCC 982

91. **Q: What is the primary purpose of the Sacrament of Reconciliation?**

A: The primary purpose of the Sacrament of Reconciliation is the forgiveness of sins committed after Baptism.

In the Bible: Sirach 18:12—13; Sirach 21:1; Acts 26:17—18
In the Catechism: CCC 1421, 1446, 1468

Going Deeper

Through Baptism we become children of God, are welcomed into a life of grace, and given the promise of heaven. As we get older, we may do things that harm our relationship with God. But God keeps loving us, and invites us to participate in regular Reconciliation so that our friendship with him can always be as strong as it was in Baptism. If we offend God, the best thing to do is to say sorry to God by going to Reconciliation.

92. **Q: What other names is the Sacrament of Reconciliation known by?**

A: In different places and different times, the Sacrament of Reconciliation is also called the Sacrament of Conversion, Confession or Penance.

In the Bible: Mark 1:15; Proverbs 28:13; Acts 3:19; 2 Peter 3:9
In the Catechism: CCC 1423, 1424

Going Deeper

Jesus loves you and he wants to save you from your sins. He wants to save you because he wants to live in friendship with you on earth and in heaven. He wants to share his joy with you and he wants you to share that joy with others. No matter what name is used, the Sacrament of Reconciliation restores our friendship with God and helps us become the-best-version-of-ourselves, grow in virtue, and live a holy life.

93. **Q: Is the Sacrament of Reconciliation a blessing?**

A: Yes, it is a great blessing from God.

In the Bible: Psalm 32: 1—2; Romans 4:6—8
In the Catechism: CCC 1468, 1496

94. **Q: Who commits sins?**

A: All people sin.

In the Bible: Romans 3:23—25; 1 John 1:8—10
In the Catechism: CCC 827

95. Q: **How can a mortal sin be forgiven?**

A: Through the Sacrament of Reconciliation.

In the Bible: 2 Corinthians 5:20–21
In the Catechism: CCC 1446, 1497

96. Q: **What is the ordinary way for someone to be reconciled with God and his Church?**

A: The ordinary way for someone to be reconciled with God and his Church is by personally confessing all grave sin to a priest followed by absolution.

In the Bible: John 20:23
In the Catechism: CCC 1497

Going Deeper

We all stray away from God from time to time. When we do, it is a good time to go to the Sacrament of Reconciliation and say sorry to God. You might be tempted to fall into the trap of thinking that your sin is too big for God to forgive. But, there is nothing you can do that will make God stop loving you. The doors of the Church are always open and God is always willing to forgive us when are sorry. The Sacrament of Reconciliation is a great blessing!

97. Q: **What three things must you do in order to receive forgiveness of sin in the Sacrament of Confession?**

A: 1. You must be truly sorry for your sins.
2. Confess all mortal sins in kind and number committed since your last confession.
3. You must resolve to amend your life.

In the Bible: Romans 8:17; Romans 3:23–26
In the Catechism: CCC 1448

Going Deeper

When we sin we become restless and unhappy. God doesn't want us to be restless and unhappy so he invites us to come to Reconciliation so that he can fill us with his joy. There may be times in your life when you feel far from God. But never think that God doesn't want you to return to him. Never think that your sins are greater than God's love. God's love and mercy will always be waiting for you in the Sacrament of Reconciliation.

98. Q: **What are the three actions required of us in the Sacrament of Reconciliation?**

A: The three actions required of us in the Sacrament of Reconciliation are:

repentance, confession of sins to the priest, and the intention to atone for our sins by performing the penance given by the priest.

In the Bible: 1 John 1:9
In the Catechism: CCC 1491

Going Deeper

Regular Reconciliation is one of the most powerful ways that God shares his grace and mercy with us. God asks us to be sorry for our sins, confess them out loud to a priest, and do an act of penance so that our friendship with God can be restored and strengthened. The more you go to Reconciliation the more you will come to realize the incredible power of God's grace and mercy in your life.

99. **Q: Who has the power to forgive sin?**

A: Jesus Christ through a Catholic priest.

In the Bible: John 20:23; 2 Corinthians 5:18
In the Catechism: CCC 1461, 1493, 1495

100. **Q: Can the priest talk about your sins with other people?**

A: No. The priest must keep secret all sins confessed to him.

In the Bible: 2 Corinthians 5:18–19
In the Catechism: CCC 1467

Going Deeper

If you are nervous about going to Confession, it's ok. Being nervous is natural. Just know that the priest is there to help you. He will not think poorly of you because of your sins or tell anyone what they are. Instead, he will be happy that you went to Confession. Remember, the priest is there to encourage you, extend God's love and mercy to you, and to help you grow in virtue.

101. **Q: What is the purpose of penance?**

A: After you have confessed your sins, the priest will propose penance for you to perform. The purpose of these acts of penance is to repair the harm caused by sin and to re-establish the habits of a disciple of Christ.

In the Bible: Luke 19:8; Acts 2:38
In the Catechism: CCC 1459–1460

Going Deeper

Friendship is beautiful but it is also fragile. God gives us the Sacrament of Reconciliation to heal the pain caused by sin and to repair our friendship with him. When we do our penance we show God that we are truly sorry. Penance helps our souls get healthy again.

102. **Q: How often should you go to Confession?**

A: You should go immediately if you are in a state of mortal sin; otherwise, it is recommended to go once a month because it is highly recommended to confess venial sins. Prior to confession you should carefully examine your conscience.

In the Bible: Acts 3:19; Luke 5:31–32; Jeremiah 31:19
In the Catechism: CCC 1457, 1458

Going Deeper

God loves healthy relationships and forgiveness is essential to having healthy relationships. Regularly going to God in the Sacrament of Reconciliation and asking for forgiveness is a powerful way to have a fabulous relationship with God. Many of the saints went to Reconciliation every month, some even more often. They knew that going to Confession was the only way to be reconciled to God. They also knew that nothing brought them more joy than having a strong friendship with Jesus.

103. **Q: Does the Sacrament of Reconciliation reconcile us only with God?**

A: No. The Sacrament of Reconciliation reconciles us with God and with the Church.

In the Bible: 1 Corinthians 12:26
In the Catechism: CCC 1422, 1449, 1469

Going Deeper

God delights in his relationship with you and he delights in your relationship with the Church. Sin makes your soul sick, it hurts other people, and it harms your relationship with God and the Church. When we go to Confession, God forgives us and heals our soul. He also heals our relationship with him and with the Church through the Sacrament of Reconciliation.

104. **Q: How do we experience God's mercy?**

A: We experience God's mercy in the Sacrament of Reconciliation. We also experience God's mercy through the kindness, generosity, and compassion of other people. God's mercy always draws us closer to him. We can also be instruments of God's mercy by exercising the works of mercy with kindness, generosity, and compassion.

In the Bible: Luke 3:11; John 8:11
In the Catechism: CCC 1422, 1449, 2447

Going Deeper

Sometimes when we do something that is wrong we may be tempted to think that God will not love us anymore. But that is never true. God will always love you because our God is a merciful God. God shows us his mercy by forgiving us, teaching us, and caring for our physical and spiritual needs even when we don't deserve it. He shows us his mercy through the Sacrament of Reconciliation and through the loving actions of other people. God invites you to spread his mercy by forgiving others, praying for others, and caring for those in need.

105. **Q: Where in the Church building is Jesus present in a special way?**

A: In the tabernacle.

In the Bible: Exodus 40:34; Luke 22:19
In the Catechism: CCC 1379

106. **Q: Who is the source of all blessings?**

A: God is the source of all blessings. In the Mass we praise and adore God the Father as the source of every blessing in creation. We also thank God the Father for sending us his Son. Most of all we express our gratitude to God the Father for making us his children.

In the Bible: Luke 1:68–79; Psalm 72:18–19
In the Catechism: CCC 1083, 1110

Going Deeper

You are blessed in so many ways. But every blessing comes from the very first blessing—life! God has given you life and made you his child. This is an incredible blessing! One of the greatest ways we can show God our gratitude is by going to Mass. By showing up every Sunday and participating in Mass, you show God how thankful you are for everything he has done for you.

107. **Q: True or False. When you receive Holy Communion, you receive a piece of bread that signifies, symbolizes, or represents Jesus.**

A: False.

In the Bible: Matthew 26:26
In the Catechism: CCC 1374, 1413

108. Q: **What do you receive in Holy Communion?**

A: The Body, Blood, Soul, and Divinity of Christ.

In the Bible: 1 Corinthians 11:24 ; John 6: 54–55
In the Catechism: CCC 1374, 1413

Going Deeper

Jesus is truly present in the Eucharist. It is not a symbol; it is Jesus. We receive all of Jesus in the Eucharist. Even the tiniest crumb that falls from the wafer contains all of Jesus. The bread and wine become Jesus at the moment of Consecration. This is an incredible moment. In this moment Jesus comes among us once again. Every time you go to Mass, bread and wine are transformed into the Body and Blood of Jesus. You are blessed to be able to receive Jesus in the Eucharist.

109. Q: **What is Transubstantiation?**

A: Transubstantiation is when the bread and wine become the Body and Blood of Jesus.

In the Bible: Matthew 26:26; Mark 14:22; Luke 22:19–20
In the Catechism: CCC 1376

Going Deeper

God has the power to transform everyone and everything he comes in contact with. Everyday, in every Catholic Church, during every Mass, God transforms ordinary bread and wine into the Body and Blood of Jesus Christ. After receiving Jesus in the Eucharist, many of the saints prayed that they would become what they had received. God answered their prayers and transformed their lives by helping them to live like Jesus. Just like with the saints, God can transform your life. Every time you receive Jesus in the Eucharist worthily, you can become a little more like him. Just like Jesus, you can love generously and serve powerfully everyone you meet.

110. Q: **When does the bread and wine change into the Body and Blood of Christ?**

A: It is changed by the words and intention of the priest at the moment of Consecration during Mass. The priest, asking for the help of the Holy Spirit, says the same words Jesus said at the Last Supper: "This is my body which will be given up for you... This is the cup of my blood..."

In the Bible: Mark 14:22; Luke 22:19–20
In the Catechism: CCC 1412, 1413

Going Deeper

The Last Supper is the most famous meal in the history of the world. In that room two thousand years ago, Jesus gave himself completely to his apostles. Every time we come to Mass, the priest recites the same words as Jesus during the Last Supper. When he does, the wheat bread and grape wine become the Body and Blood of Jesus. Amazing! Jesus wants to give himself completely to you just as he gave himself completely to his apostles at the Last Supper. Jesus wants to be invited into your life. He wants to encourage you, guide you, listen to you, and love you. He offers himself to you in a special way at Mass, especially in the amazing gift of Holy Communion.

111. **Q: What are the benefits of receiving the Body and Blood of Jesus in the Eucharist?**

    A: When you receive Jesus in the Eucharist you become more united with the Lord, your venial sins are forgiven, and you are given grace to avoid grave sins. Receiving Jesus in the Eucharist also increases your love for Jesus and reinforces the fact that you are a member of God's family — the Catholic Church.

    In the Bible: John 6:56–57
    In the Catechism: CCC 1391–1396

Going Deeper

The Eucharist empowers us to do great things for God. The saints did incredible things for God throughout their lives and the Eucharist was the source of their strength. Through Holy Communion we grow closer to God, move further away from sinful habits, and grow in love for Jesus and the Catholic Church. The Eucharist is the ultimate food for your soul and it will give you the strength and courage to serve God and others powerfully just like the saints.

112. **Q: How important is the Eucharist to the life of the Church?**

    A: The Eucharist is indispensable in the life of the Church. The Eucharist is the heart of the Church. One of the reasons the Eucharist is so important to the life of the Church is because, through it, Jesus unites every member of the Church with his sacrifice on the cross. Every grace that flows from Jesus' suffering, death, and Resurrection comes to us through the Church.

    In the Bible: John 6:51, 54, 56
    In the Catechism: CCC 1324, 1331, 1368, 1407

Going Deeper

Jesus promised to be with us always, no matter what. He has been keeping this promise for over 2,000 years. Jesus is always with us in the Eucharist. The Eucharist unites us to Jesus and his Church. It also unites us to one another. We are blessed to have the Eucharist. Only through the Catholic Church can we receive the gift of the Eucharist. We are blessed to be Catholic.

113. Q: **Should you receive Holy Communion in the state of mortal sin?**

A: No. If you do, you commit the additional mortal sin of sacrilege.

In the Bible: 1 Corinthians 11:27–29
In the Catechism: CCC 1385, 1415, 1457

Going Deeper

If Jesus came to visit your home and it was so messy you couldn't open the door to let Jesus in, that would be terrible. No matter how much Jesus wants to be a part of our lives he will never force himself upon us. Mortal sin slams the door of our souls in Jesus' face. It breaks our relationship with God and prevents the wonderful graces of the Eucharist from flowing into our hearts, minds, and souls. Reconciliation reopens the door to our souls and let's Jesus enter our lives again.

114. Q: **What is sacrilege?**

A: It is the abuse of a sacred person, place, or thing.

In the Bible: 1 Corinthians 11:27–29
In the Catechism: CCC 2120

115. Q: **If you are in a state of mortal sin, what should you do before receiving Holy Communion?**

A: You should go to Confession as soon as possible.

In the Bible: 2 Corinthians 5:20
In the Catechism: CCC 1385, 1457

116. Q: **Who offered the first Mass?**

A: Jesus Christ.

In the Bible: Mark 14:22–24
In the Catechism: CCC 1323

117. Q: **When did Jesus offer the first Mass?**

A: On Holy Thursday night, the night before He died, at the Last Supper.

In the Bible: Matthew 26:26—28
In the Catechism: CCC 1323

118. Q: Who offers the Eucharistic sacrifice?

A: Jesus is the eternal high priest. In the Mass, he offers the Eucharistic sacrifice through the ministry of the priest.

In the Bible: Mark 14:22; Matthew 26:26; Luke 22:19; 1 Corinthians 11:24;
In the Catechism: CCC 1348

Going Deeper

The Last Supper was the first Eucharistic celebration. This was the apostles First Communion, and the first time anybody had ever received the Eucharist. The Mass is not just a symbol of what happened that night. Jesus is truly present in the Eucharist. Every time we receive Holy Communion Jesus gives himself to us in the same way he gave himself to his apostles over 2,000 years ago. Jesus works through the priest at Mass to transform the bread and wine into his Body and Blood.

119. Q: What is the Sacrifice of the Mass?

A: It is the sacrifice of Jesus Christ on Calvary, the memorial of Christ's Passover, made present when the priest repeats the words of Consecration spoken by Jesus over the bread and wine at the Last Supper.

In the Bible: Hebrews 7:25—27
In the Catechism: CCC 1364, 1413

Going Deeper

God loves you so much and he will go to unimaginable lengths to prove his love for you. On Good Friday Jesus was beaten, bullied, mocked, spat upon, cursed at, and crucified on the cross. Jesus laid down his life for us. On Easter Sunday Jesus rose from the dead. He did this so that we might live a very different life while here on earth and happily with him forever in heaven. Every time we go to Mass we remember the life of Jesus, the path he invites us to walk, and the incredible lengths he went to show us his love.

120. Q: Who can preside at the Eucharist?

A: Only an ordained priest can preside at the Eucharist and Consecrate the bread and the wine so that they become the Body and Blood of Jesus.

In the Bible: John 13:3—8
In the Catechism: CCC 1411

Going Deeper

To be a priest is a great honor and privilege. Priests lay down their lives to serve God and his people. The priesthood is a life of service. One of the ultimate privileges of the priesthood is standing in Jesus' place and transforming bread and wine into the Eucharist. This privilege is reserved for priests alone. Nobody other than a priest can do this.

121. **Q: How do we participate in the Sacrifice of the Mass?**

A: By uniting ourselves and our intentions to the bread and wine, offered by the priest, which become Jesus' sacrifice to the Father.

In the Bible: Romans 12:1
In the Catechism: CCC 1407

122. **Q: What does the Eucharistic celebration we participate in at Mass always include?**

A: The Eucharist celebration always includes: the proclamation of the Word of God; thanksgiving to God the Father for all his blessings; the Consecration of the bread and wine; and participation in the liturgical banquet by receiving the Lord's Body and Blood. These elements constitute one single act of worship.

In the Bible: Luke 24:13–35
In the Catechism: CCC 1345–1355, 1408

Going Deeper

The Mass follows a certain formula that is always repeated and never changes. You could go to Mass anywhere in the world and you will always find it is the same. At every Mass we read from the Bible, show God our gratitude for the blessing of Jesus, witness bread and wine transformed into the Body and Blood of Jesus, and receive Jesus during Holy Communion. In the midst of this great routine, God wants to surprise you. You could spend a lifetime going to Mass every single day and at the end of your life still be surprised by what God has to say to you in the Mass. The Mass is truly amazing!

123. **Q: What role does music play in the Mass?**

A: Sacred music helps us to worship God.

In the Bible: Ps 57:8–10; Ephesians 5:19; Hebrews 2:12; Colossians 3:16;
In the Catechism: CCC 1156

Going Deeper

Sometimes when we are praying it can be difficult to find the right words to express how we feel. To help us, God gives us the great gift of sacred music. Over the course of the Mass there will be songs of praise, songs of worship, songs of petition, and songs of thanksgiving. Sacred music helps raise our hearts to God and bond us together as a community calling out to God with one voice.

124. **Q: What is the Lord's Day?**

A: Sunday is the Lord's Day. It is a day of rest. It is a day to gather as a family. It is the principal day for celebrating the Eucharist because it is the day of the Resurrection.

In the Bible: Exodus 31:15; Matthew 28:1; Mark 16:2; John 20:1;
In the Catechism: CCC 1166; 1193; 2174

Going Deeper

Sunday is a very special day. The Resurrection of Jesus is so important that we celebrate it every day at Mass. But we celebrate the Resurrection of Jesus in a special way every Sunday. We do that by resting, spending time with family, and going to Mass. The Lord's Day is a day to marvel at all the amazing ways God has blessed us, and because of that it is a day of gratitude.

125. **Q: Is it a mortal sin for you to miss Mass on Sunday or a Holy Day through your own fault?**

A: Yes.

In the Bible: Exodus 20:8
In the Catechism: CCC 2181

126. **Q: Which person of the Holy Trinity do you receive in Confirmation?**

A: The Holy Spirit.

In the Bible: Romans 8:15
In the Catechism: CCC 1302

127. **Q: What happens in the Sacrament of Confirmation?**

A: The Holy Spirit comes upon us and strengthens us to be soldiers of Christ that we may spread and defend the Catholic faith.

In the Bible: John 14:26; 15:26
In the Catechism: CCC 1303, 2044

128. Q: What is Confirmation?

A: Confirmation is a Sacrament that perfects Baptismal grace. Through it we receive the Holy Spirit and are strengthened in grace so we can grow in virtue, live holy lives, and carry out the mission God calls us to.

In the Bible: John 20:22; Acts 2:1–4
In the Catechism: CCC: 1285, 1316

Going Deeper

When you are older you will be blessed to receive the Sacrament of Confirmation. Confirmation reminds us that in Baptism God blessed us with a special mission and filled us with the Holy Spirit. Through an outpouring of the Holy Spirit at Confirmation, we are filled with the courage and wisdom to live out the mission God has given us. Confirmation deepens our friendship with Jesus and the Catholic Church. It reminds us that we are sons and daughters of a great King. It will be a special moment in your life and a wonderful blessing!

129. Q: When is Confirmation received?

A: Most Catholics in the West receive Confirmation during their teenage years, but in the East Confirmation is administered immediately after Baptism.

In the Bible: Hebrews 6:1–3
In the Catechism: CCC 1306, 1318

Going Deeper

Baptism, Confirmation and First Holy Communion are called the Sacraments of Initiation. In a special way, the Sacraments of Initiation deepen our friendship with Jesus and the Church, fill us with what we need to live out God's mission for our lives, and inspire us to become all that God created us to be. It is important to remember that these three Sacraments are connected. They are the foundation for a fabulous friendship with God on earth and forever in heaven. In some parts of the world, and at different times throughout history, people have received these Sacraments at different times according to local traditions and practical considerations. For example, hundreds of years ago, the bishop may have only visited a village once every two or three years, and so Confirmation would take place when he visited. Even today, some children receive Baptism, First Communion, and Confirmation all at the same time.

130. Q: What are the Seven Gifts of the Holy Spirit?

A: Wisdom, understanding, counsel, fortitude, knowledge, piety, and fear of the Lord.

In the Bible: Isaiah 11:2–3
In the Catechism: CCC 1830, 1831

131. Q: **Before you are confirmed, you will promise the bishop that you will never give up the practice of your Catholic faith for anyone or anything. Did you ever make that promise before?**

A: Yes, at Baptism.

In the Bible: Joshua 24:21–22
In the Catechism: CCC 1298

132. Q: **Most of you were baptized as little babies. How could you make that promise?**

A: Our parents and godparents made that promise for us.

In the Bible: Mark 16:16
In the Catechism: CCC 1253

133. Q: **What kind of sin is it to receive Confirmation in the state of mortal sin?**

A: A sacrilege.

In the Bible: 1 Corinthians 11:27–29
In the Catechism: CCC 2120

134. Q: **If you have committed mortal sin, what should you do before receiving Confirmation?**

A: You should make a good Confession.

In the Bible: 2 Corinthians 5:20; Luke 15:18
In the Catechism: CCC 1310

135. Q: **What are the three traditional vocations?**

A: Married life, Holy Orders, and the consecrated life.

In the Bible: Ephesians 5:31–32; Hebrews 5:6, 7:11; Ps 110:4; Matthew 19:12; 1 Corinthians 7:34–66
In the Catechism: CCC 914, 1536, 1601

136. Q: **What are the three vows that a consecrated man or woman takes?**

A: Chastity, Poverty, and Obedience.

In the Bible: Matthew 19:21; Matthew 19:12; 1 Corinthians 7:34–36; Hebrews 10:7;
In the Catechism: CCC 915

137. **Q: What are the three ranks (degrees) of Holy Orders?**
A: Deacon, Priest, and Bishop.

> In the Bible: 1 Timothy 4:14; 2 Timothy 1:6–7
> In the Catechism: CCC 1554

138. **Q: For whom did God make marriage?**
A: One man and one woman.

> In the Bible: Genesis 1:26–28; Ephesians 5:31
> In the Catechism: CCC 1601, 2360

139. **Q: Is it possible for two men or two women to get married?**
A: No.

> In the Bible: Genesis 19:1–29; Romans 1:24–27; 1 Corinthians 6:9;
> In the Catechism: CCC 2357, 2360

140. **Q: When can a man and woman begin living together?**
A: Only after their marriage.

> In the Bible: 1 Corinthians 6:18–20
> In the Catechism: CCC 235

141. **Q: What are the three marriage promises a husband and wife make to each other?**
A: Faithfulness, permanence, and being open to having children.

> In the Bible: Matthew 19:6; Genesis 1:28
> In the Catechism: CCC 1640, 1641, 1664

142. **Q: Why is abortion wrong?**
A: Because it takes the life of a baby in its mother's womb.

> In the Bible: Jeremiah 1:5; Psalm 139:13
> In the Catechism: CCC 2270

143. **Q: How many commandments are there?**
A: Ten.

> In the Bible: Exodus 20:1–18; Deuteronomy 5:6–21
> In the Catechism: CCC 2054

144. **Q: What are the Ten Commandments?**

A: 1. I, the Lord, am your God. You shall not have other gods besides me.
2. You shall not take the name of the Lord, your God, in vain.
3. Remember to keep holy the Lord's Day.
4. Honor your father and mother.
5. You shall not kill.
6. You shall not commit adultery.
7. You shall not steal.
8. You shall not bear false witness against your neighbor.
9. You shall not covet your neighbor's wife.
10. You shall not covet your neighbor's goods.

In the Bible: Exodus 20:1–18; Deuteronomy 5:6–21
In the Catechism: CCC 496, 497

145. **Q: What are the four main kinds of prayer?**

A: The four main kinds of prayer are adoration, thanksgiving, petition, and intercession.

In the Bible: Ps 95:6; Colossians 4:2; James 5:16; 1 John 3:22
In the Catechism: CCC 2628, 2629, 2634, 2638, 2639

146. **Q: How often should we pray?**

A: Every day.

In the Bible: 1 Thessalonians 5:17; Luke 18:1
In the Catechism: CCC 2742

Acknowledgments

This project began with a dream: to create the best First Reconciliation and First Communion experience in the world. For the millions of young souls that will experience this program we hope we have delivered on that dream.

Hundreds of people have poured their time, talent, and expertise into *Blessed*. It is the result of years of research, development, and testing. To everyone who has contributed—and you know who you are—in every stage of the process: Thank You! May God bless you and reward you richly for your generosity.

Special thanks to: Jack Beers, Bridget Eichold, Katie Ferrara, Allen and Anita Hunt, Steve Lawson, Mark Moore, Shawna Navaro, Father Robert Sherry, and Ben Skudlarek.

Beyond the enormous talent contributions, others have been incredibly generous with their money. *Blessed* was funded by a group of incredibly generous donors. It will now be made available at no cost to every parish in North America. This is one of the many ways that this program is unique.

Everything great in history has been accomplished by people who believed that the future could be better than the past. Thank you for believing!

Now we offer *Blessed* to the Church as a gift, hopeful that it will help young Catholics encounter Jesus and discover the genius of Catholicism.

Blessed was:

Written by: Matthew Kelly
Illustrated by: Carolina Farias
Designed by: The Dynamic Catholic Design Team
Principal designers: Ben Hawkins and Jenny Miller

Help *Blessed* become The-Best-Version-of-Itself

Blessed is different from other programs in a hundred ways. One way that it is different is that it is always changing and improving. We need your help with this. Whether you find a typo or think of some fun way to improve the program, please email us and tell us about it so that year after year *Blessed* can become even more dynamic.

blessed@dynamiccatholic.com

Blessed

The Dynamic Catholic First Communion Experience
©2017 The Dynamic Catholic Institute and Kakadu, LLC.

The Scripture quotations contained herein are from *The Catholic Edition of the Revised Standard Version Bible*, copyright © 1965, 1966 by the Division of Christian Education of the National Council of the Churches of Christ in the U.S.A., and are used by permission.

This volume contains quotes and excerpts from a number of titles previously released by Matthew Kelly. The copyright to these works are held by Beacon Publishing. These quotes and excerpts have been made available to Dynamic Catholic for use in this volume, but the copyright to these quotes and excerpts remains the property of Beacon Publishing.

Dynamic Catholic®. Be Bold. Be Catholic.® and The-Best-Version-of-Yourself® are registered trademarks of the Dynamic Catholic Institute.

ISBN 978-1-929266-44-9

FIRST EDITION

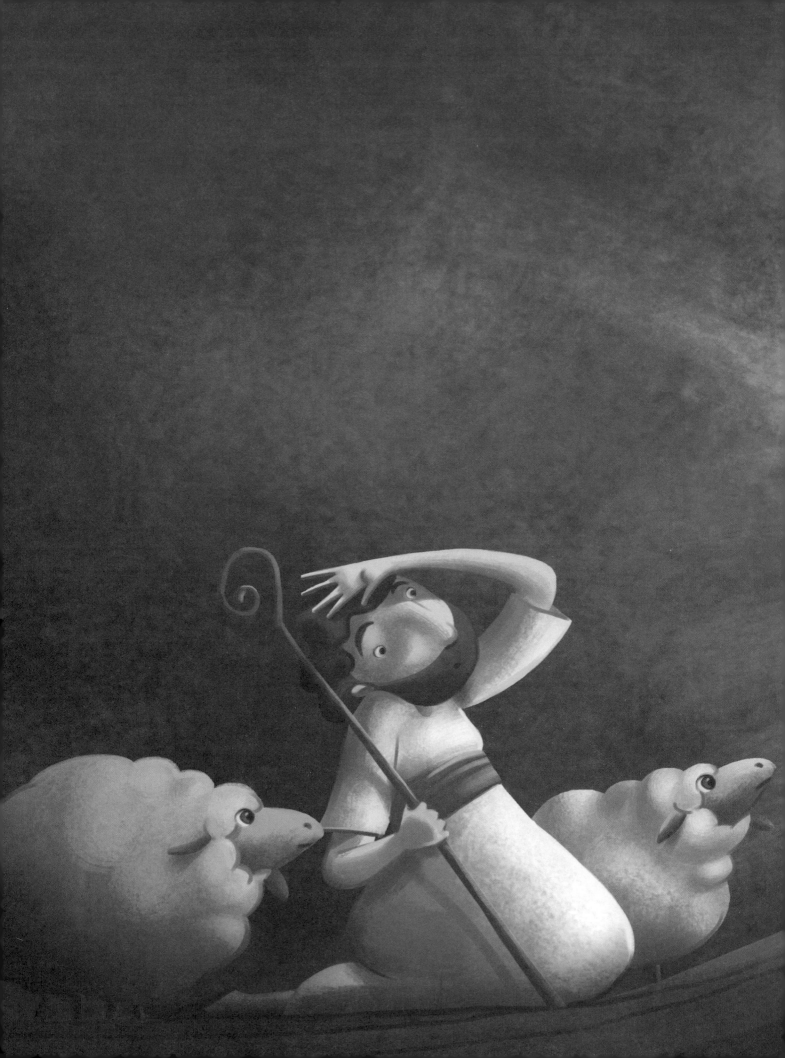